THE NATURE OF SAINT JOHN'S

 # SAINT JOHN'S ABBEY

Saint John's Abbey of Collegeville, Minnesota, is a community of Catholic Benedictine men who seek God through a common life of prayer, study, and work, giving witness to Christ and the Gospel, serving the church and the world. The second-largest Benedictine Abbey in the Western Hemisphere, it was founded in 1856 by monks from Saint Vincent Archabbey in Latrobe, Pennsylvania, and is affiliated with the American-Cassinese Congregation.

Saint John's Abbey Arboretum is more than 2,500 acres of lakes, prairie, oak savanna, and forest, owned by Saint John's Abbey.

COLLEGE OF
Saint Benedict ✚ Saint John's
UNIVERSITY

Saint John's University (SJU), for men, and the *College of Saint Benedict* (CSB), for women, are partner, residential liberal arts colleges in the Catholic Benedictine tradition. Their campuses, three and a half miles apart, are in central Minnesota. The graduate programs of Saint John's School of Theology and Seminary educate men and women for ordained and lay ministry in the church.

Saint John's Outdoor University (Outdoor U) provides outdoor and environmental education through classes, events, and initiatives with the Abbey Arboretum, Saint John's University, and the College of Saint Benedict.

The Nature
of Saint John's

*A Guide to the Landscape and Spirituality
of Saint John's Abbey Arboretum*

Edited by Larry Haeg
with Jennifer Kutter

SAINT JOHN'S UNIVERSITY PRESS
COLLEGEVILLE, MINNESOTA

*Saint John's University Press publishes
distinctive work that illuminates the
creative spirit of the communities of
Saint John's and the College of Saint Benedict.*

All proceeds from sales of this book support Saint John's Abbey Arboretum and Saint John's Outdoor University.

Cover design by Ann Blattner. Front cover photo courtesy of Deanna Jansky; back cover photo courtesy of Jerry Furst.

Interior book design by Julie Surma.

1	2	3	4	5	6	7	8

Library of Congress Cataloging-in-Publication Data

The nature of Saint John's : a guide to the landscape and spirituality of Saint John's Abbey Arboretum / Larry Haeg, managing editor.

      pages   cm
  Includes index.
  ISBN 978-0-9884075-0-3 — ISBN 978-0-9884075-4-1 (ebook)
  1. St. John's Abbey (Collegeville, Minn.). Arboretum.   2. Natural history—Minnesota—Collegeville.   3. Nature trails—Minnesota—Collegeville.   4. Nature—Religious aspects.   I. Haeg, Larry, Jr., 1945–

QK480.U52S72   2015
508.776'47—dc23   2015002165

In memory of
Father Paul Schwietz, O.S.B. (1952–2000),
dedicated conservationist and Abbey forester, 1985–2000

"There is a holiness to nature, in the intricacy of the
system. Its secrets are open to all to learn, but it takes patience
to develop the eyes and history necessary to see."

Contents

The *Rule of Saint Benedict* and Environmental Stewardship

I grew up on a family farm about forty-five miles west of Saint John's. We spent a significant amount of time driving our tractor over the fields, plowing, cultivating, planting, and harvesting. We got to know fields in a specific way, what grew well, where it might be too wet to drive, where pheasants might hide. My dad was careful about ditching and created grass waterways for runoff, to minimize erosion. He was constantly seeking to improve the tilth and fertility of the soil. In a fundamental way, I was learning about the positive relationship we as human beings have with the environment, that we as human beings are connected to the birds, the sloughs, the wetlands, the prairies, and the forest for the long haul.

Coming to Saint John's as a young lad allowed me to continue this theme of stability and personal engagement in caring for the environment. A few weeks after coming to campus as a first-year prep student in 1963, I was invited to work on a Saturday putting in a small culvert on the pathway to the Stella Maris Chapel. The five of us worked all afternoon installing that culvert, situating it properly, and then filling around it with dirt and other material, packing it in to make the trail safer for walking and running. As prep students we often walked and ran this trail because it is especially beautiful as it wraps around Lake Sagatagan. Because of its proximity to the lake and the forest, the landscape was a constant part of our awareness.

Grounded in a Place

As a monk of Saint John's Abbey since 1971, I have come to realize that Benedictine stability has to include both a commitment to a specific place and a commitment to a specific group of people. If you go to a place and there is no *there*, there, it's not a Benedictine place! I don't know what it is, but it is *not* Benedictine.

Exploring, studying, seeing the place where one lives leads to a deep knowledge and love for the local environment and grounds one in a place. Of course, there are examples of communities that have destroyed their own local habitat. In the first seven thousand years of agriculture, overgrazing was one of the single most damaging practices that caused large tracts of land to be badly eroded or converted into desert. Human ignorance or the inability to change destructive practices can wreak havoc in any situation.

By coming to know a place deeply—the overlapping ecosystems, the delicate balance among the number of creatures and available nourishment, the patterns that play themselves out year after year—monastic communities try to make decisions with an understanding of their consequences. In the event of a serious mistake, the community will be around long enough to recognize it as such. Evidence tells us our Abbey has always designated someone to see that we harvest timber on Abbey land in a way that regenerates the forest.

This is not an argument against change but an argument for environmental knowledge. It is a knowledge that will lead us to recognize the habitats that are necessary for different kinds of wildlife. It will draw us to learn something about the original forest, to review topography and soil and climate conditions, and reforest if necessary. It is an argument for "wildness," for resisting the temptation to create places where there are no tall grasses, fallen trees, and piles of leaves for animals to dwell. I think this kind of knowledge changes us and the kind of education we want to give to our students.

The Natural World as a Wisdom Book

The *Rule of Benedict* is a wisdom book. In an understated way it offers a pathway to live the Gospel. The natural world is also a wisdom book, however, one that can be read, pondered, prayed, and contemplated. The earth can also teach us about our lives. All too often we think of other humans as our primary teachers. But the earth can teach us about change in a unique way because it has a four-billion-year résumé in the field. The earth can teach us about loss and grief, about death and transformation. It is a great learning experience to walk a favorite path in the woods, to stop in favorite places, to do so in each of the seasons, and to note how the place changes with the seasons. Likewise, while praying in the Abbey Church, designed by Marcel Breuer, we are connected to the changing light of day and the seasons. We are aware of the passage of time.

Nature has much to teach about human limits, the seasons of a person's life, the cycle of death and renewal. This learning is reinforced in our prayer because the psalms and the Scriptures are loaded with imagery from the natural world, and this is activated in a fresh and powerful way by firsthand knowledge of the environment in which we live. We come to know ourselves as part of the created world and not in opposition to it.

The earth teaches us about the cycle of life and death. Acknowledging the reality of death reorients the meaning of human life. In his *Rule*, Saint Benedict is specific about death. He urges the monk to keep death daily before his eyes (RB 4.47). Many of the psalms are embedded with a haunting sense of the fragility and finitude of human living and striving. Life is a gift, a given span of days, seventy years, or eighty for those who are strong (Ps 90:10). So also the Abbey Arboretum and this campus are gifts, to be received with joy and care, to be a part of for a while, then handed to the next generation.

The Music of Nature

Sitting in a secluded place by Lake Sagatagan off Pickerel Point, I gradually become part of the symphony. There is the steady ebb and flow of the waves, the graceful refrain of the wind, the slaphappy dance of the leaves, the cumulus clouds folding and turning through the sky. Music was not invented when some long-ago composer decided to blow through a hollow reed or tap an empty seedpod. It began long before our species. Much music is based on nature's sense of rhythm, harmonics, tone, and cadence. One of my favorite characters in Tolstoy's *War and Peace* is Platon Karataev, who "sang songs, not as singers do, who know they are listened to, but sang, as the birds sing, obviously because it was necessary to him to utter those sounds, as it sometimes is to stretch or to walk about."

We know the Abbey Arboretum is the work, the labor of many hands, many imaginations, that managing the forest is both a science and an art, that replanting a hardwood forest is an arduous task, trying to stay ahead of those pesky deer! We of Saint John's Abbey and our extended community are grateful for the sheer beauty and diversity of the natural environment of this place that is so central to what it means to be associated with Saint John's.

We pray it is so for you.

Abbot John Klassen, O.S.B.

> O Lord, how manifold are your works!
> In wisdom you have made them all;
> the earth is full of your creatures.

—Psalm 104:24

There is a nobility in the duty to care for creation through little daily actions, and it is wonderful how education can bring about real changes in lifestyle. Education in environmental responsibility can encourage ways of acting which directly and significantly affect the world around us.

—Pope Francis, *Laudato Sì*, no. 211

Teach us to discover the worth of each thing,
to be filled with awe and contemplation,
to recognize that we are profoundly united
with every creature
as we journey towards your infinite light.
We thank you for being with us each day.
Encourage us, we pray, in our struggle
For justice, love and peace.

—Pope Francis, *Laudato Sì*, Prayer for Our Earth

Genesis

In the beginning when God created the heavens and the earth, the earth was a formless void and darkness covered the face of the deep.

—Genesis 1:1

How God Shaped This Land

The 2,500 acres of Saint John's landscape were shaped over eons by volcanoes, sediment from sea beds, and the folding of tectonic plates, forming mountains that glaciers scraped away during some two million years.

Our landscape today is defined by "terminal end moraines." They were shaped by the southward advance of glaciers, offset by melting. This created a "conveyer belt" that deposited rock and soil from the north and west. When the glaciers retreated north, they left the Avon Hills landscape with rolling hills of silt, sand, and clay. This unusual churning of earth is known as glacial till, and it makes what's beneath the surface very unpredictable. Land west of Saint John's was largely scraped into flat plains. To the south, glaciers either scraped land flat or left it untouched. The glaciers that had the most effect on Saint John's landscape were the Wisconsin lobe (11,000 to 30,000 years ago), the Wadena lobe (about 30,000 years ago), and the Rainy and Superior lobes (some 20,500 years ago).

Water drained from lakes the size of seas, formed by melting glaciers, and rain wore away the land. Streams and rivers formed channels toward the lowest points in the landscape. At Saint John's, this flow of water formed the North Fork of the Watab* River which meets the south fork north of Saint Joseph. The Watab River flows north and east from there through Sartell and into the Mississippi River. Depressions left by slow-melting blocks of glacial ice form most of the lakes and "potholes" that jewel our landscape.

The Stones of Saint John's

Like living stones, let yourselves be built into a spiritual house.
—1 Peter 2:5

Glacial till holds a vast rubble of limestone and gravel sands, cobbles and boulders of basalt, gabbro, granite, gneiss, red sandstone, slate, and greenstone. These boulders and cobblestone may look like what retired geology professor Larry E. Davis called "chaotic amalgamations," but each one can be  traced to a specific source based on its distinctive minerals.

The pioneer monks of Saint John's gathered these fieldstones and boulders from the fields and used them to form the three-foot-thick foundation of the Quadrangle and original Abbey Church (1888). Inspired by Abbot Alcuin Deutsch, O.S.B., after one of his trips to Europe, monks such as Joachim

* Ojibwe for long, slender roots of tamarack and jack pine used to sew birch bark canoes.

Watrin, O.S.B., and Arno Gustin, O.S.B., helped build field stone structures in the early 1930s such as the stone walls around the monastic gardens, the walls around Saint Francis House, the Old Stone Gate, and the original steps leading down to Clemens Stadium football field. There also is local granite in the stone pavers (1961) at the entrance to the world-renowned Saint John's Abbey and University Church. Master stone-mason John Pueringer, whose land "produced better stones than corn" helped guide the monks' work. He knew "where a crack with the stone hammer could split a stone," wrote Father Alfred Deutsch, O.S.B.; "he knew the edges of stone, and how they would rest; he knew how to tuck back the binding cement so that the joints of stone folded into each other."

The Ojibwe and Dakota Legacy

One way we understand landscape is through the eyes of those who came before us. Human beings hunted and gathered where Saint John's stands now shortly after the glaciers receded. There is, however, no record of a major indigenous settlement here, perhaps because the Saint John's watershed doesn't directly connect to any major navigable waterway.

Over the last 300 years, the long-established Dakota tribes were displaced from this region by the Ojibwe, who were pushed from their eastern lands by white settlements. Through a series of treaties drawn by the US government, borders between these two tribes shifted several times before settling under American control in 1851, moving the Ojibwe to reservations in northern Minnesota. In 1825 the Dakota and Ojibwe agreed to a north-south boundary with the US government, dividing the two tribes. This boundary ran up the Mississippi River, then up the Watab River, following the North Fork of the

Watab River to its supposed source at Island Lake. The boundary ran west-northwest to where Minnesota today meets North Dakota and South Dakota. The federal government assigned the Ojibwe the land north and east of this line, the Dakota south and west. This put present-day Saint John's on both sides of this border. Today's Flynntown was on the Ojibwe side and Clemens Stadium on the Dakota side, but both tribes ignored the boundary.

In 1837 the Dakota and Ojibwe surrendered parts of their north-south divide in exchange for cash, annuities, and technical help in farming. The Dakota never received any annual investment income as promised. The 1837 treaty opened part of eastern Minnesota along the Mississippi near Saint Paul and north to Mille Lacs to white settlers. In 1851 the Dakota and Ojibwe in the Treaty of Traverse des Sioux ceded the southern half of the Minnesota Territory, including present-day Saint John's. In 1855, US treaties with the Ojibwe provided for reservations in central and northern Minnesota, but after the 1862 Dakota war, the United States closed five of these reservations and the Ojibwe had to live on even less land. Because the Ojibwe controlled the area during the overlap of European settlement, most indigenous place names at Saint John's are from their language.

The Europeans Come

Europeans who came to central Minnesota in the 1600s were mostly French fur traders who followed waterways and traded with Native Americans. By the mid-1800s, Minnesota had been settled for the expansive timber harvest in the north, and later for the fertile farmland opening up to the west for Europeans, as the federal government "displaced" Native Americans to reservations.

Central Minnesota attracted a large number of Catholics, especially German Catholics gathered by the missionary Francis X. Pierz, who called for more priests to join him ministering to the immigrants. The Benedictines in Latrobe, Pennsylvania, responded by sponsoring a monastic community in our region. Five Benedictines arrived in 1856, settling on the Mississippi River in Saint Cloud. Two years later they moved to Saint Joseph, and a year later returned to Saint Cloud. A lawsuit meant they lacked clear title to the Saint Cloud site, so again they headed west. They raised a two-story frame building in a clearing on a knoll about a quarter-mile north of the present footbridge over Interstate 94. Then they moved once more, in 1866, to Saint John's current location on the shore of Lake Sagatagan.

In their early letters the Benedictines called this land "Indianbush," the glacially shaped hills west of the Mississippi left unclaimed by pioneer farmers looking for flat, more fertile land to the west and south. The first monks also called this the *Schoenthal* or "Beautiful Valley." They cleared trees for pasture and farmland and milled the trees into lumber for the remarkable buildings they envisioned. The land still bears some of the original Norway spruce, planted by the monks in the 1890s near what is now Saint John's Preparatory School. These trees never were harvested, though most of the original forest was cleared and regenerated through selective or widespread cutting.

Changing Landscape

Saint John's stands in a thin band of predominantly hardwood forest that runs from the northwest to southeast corner of Minnesota, with oceans of prairie stretching south and west toward the Rocky Mountains. Depending on climate, fire, and the roaming patterns of bison herds over thousands of years, this place has leaned deeper into the hardwood forest band to the north or further into the western prairie. When the Benedictines arrived, the wide flat expanse of what is now the prairie was still thick with trees.

We know why the Benedictines came, but why did they choose to stay? For fifteen centuries, Benedictines have believed a community of monks is more likely to find God if it stays in one place and takes care of that place. The alternative, as Benedict says in his *Rule*, is being "always on the move, with no stability" where one is tempted to "succumb to the allurements of gluttony." Rooted to the earth, Benedictine monks had to be responsible, and practical, stewards because they relied on the land for their daily needs. That requires work, frugality, stewardship, and humility (from *humus*, earth). Monks are truly monks, says the *Rule*, "when they live by the labor of their hands" (RB 48.8). Benedictines anchor themselves to the land in this way as a community and are known as cenobites (from the Greek *koinos bios* for "common life").

Thus, when the Benedictines bought claims on what was known as "Indianbush" (former hunting ground of the Ojibwe and the Dakota), they had to cultivate the land for food and fuel. They cut down trees to plant crops and create pasture. They dammed the Watab River for a sawmill. They built a brickyard, blacksmith shop, slaughterhouse, reservoir, and laundry. There was a cattle barn just west of where Sexton Commons now stands. At one time in the early twentieth century they had some one hundred head of registered Holsteins, and some steers and calves, so highly prized for their blood lines that buyers came from across central Minnesota when young bulls were offered for sale. The monks also raised sheep, chickens, and hogs. They plowed the fields with horses, then tractors, then mechanical harvesters. They raised wheat for bread, and corn and hay for livestock. They logged the hardwood forest for fuel and timber and grew rye, barley, and oats. They cleared hundreds of acres of maple and basswood for pasture, draining acres of wetland between what is now Interstate 94 and County Road 159.* Cattle grazed this man-made hay meadow for some one hundred years, removing the herbaceous species. The land was fallow for another thirty years.

The Land Around Saint John's: Avon Hills

The Avon Hills landscape—eighty square miles, including Avon, Collegeville, Saint Joseph, and Saint Wendel—has the highest concentration of native plant communities in Stearns County. The Nature Conservancy (TNC) identified it as "ecologically significant" as a part of its continent-wide search for "Last Great Places" because it's one of the few areas in the nation with intact, native plant communities. "This isn't just a local concern," said Garth Fuller of the TNC. "This place really does have global significance; it has features important both for North American and worldwide conservation efforts." The Minnesota Land Trust partners with Saint John's Abbey Arboretum to work voluntarily with landowners to create conservation easements in the Avon Hills. Collegeville Township requires developers who want to divide land into parcels smaller than twenty acres to submit a plan to protect at least fifty percent of the parcel for preservation.

---

* To preserve the forest and lessen the need for more farmland on Abbey land, the Abbey in 1881 bought a thousand acres in West Union, forty miles northwest of the monastery, for grain and hay, and sold it in 1901.

Forester Monk

Father Paul Schwietz, O.S.B. (1952–2000), was born in Saint Paul and enrolled at Saint John's University in 1971. After receiving his bachelor's degree in biology, he entered Saint John's Abbey, was ordained a priest in 1982, and received his master's degree in forestry from the University of Minnesota. Abbot Jerome Theisen, O.S.B., named him the Abbey's land manager in 1985. Father Paul then proposed a ten-year forest management plan for Saint John's. He directed an inventory of 1,300 acres of hardwood trees and the documenting of watersheds, including five hundred acres of lakes.

He planned and supervised the planting of 30,000 conifers and the thinning of thirty acres of pine plantation, some of which were the oldest in Minnesota, seeded by the monks in 1896. In the 1980s he envisioned the Habitat Restoration Project. To be consistent with Saint John's Master Plan, he and his team landscaped the inner campus with shade trees and flower gardens that provide brilliant splashes of color in spring and summer. He promoted classes in plant taxonomy, botany, bird identification, ecology, and aquatic biology. In the mid-1990s he visited several monasteries in central Europe to study their land use, including Kremsmünster Abbey, founded in 777, whose forest in the upper mountains of Austria has a rotation length between planting and final harvest of two hundred years. For his efforts to restore the Saint John's landscape to its natural state, he received the Bronze Medal award from the Minnesota Horticultural Society in 1996.

One of Father Paul's favorite prayers was Psalm 1:3, which likens God's people to "trees planted by streams of water, which yield their fruit in its season, and their leaves do not wither." He died suddenly of heart failure in May 2000 at the age of forty-seven. There is a memorial to him in the Abbey Arboretum's oak savanna. "One must approach ecological work with an element of humility," he wrote. "We don't fully understand the relationship between plants . . . and animals. The intricate web of life is a system of interdependent parts. . . . The goal is to develop a healthy, mature, and sustainable ecosystem with both sun and shade lovers. It is a new science."

The Saint John's Bible: Native Species

Early in 2000, months before he died, Father Paul walked the prairie and forest of Saint John's with Donald Jackson, the British calligrapher and artistic director of *The Saint John's Bible*. They began to identify native species of insects, plants, and animals in the Abbey Arboretum to communicate the holiness of the place and the nature of Saint John's in the first completely handwritten, hand-illuminated Bible commissioned by a Benedictine abbey since the invention of the printing press. They focused on species with biblical echoes such as vines, deer, and cranes, but took some poetic license. American crows in the Bible's illustrations became

ravens. The great blue heron substituted for the biblical stork. The monarch butterfly, rendered by Chris Tomlin for the end of the Gospel of Mark, is known for its three stages—caterpillar, chrysalis, and butterfly—biblical symbols of life, death, and resurrection. Butterflies, wrote Susan Sink in *The Art of the Saint John's Bible*, are "special creatures that bridge heaven and earth . . . often hard to keep in our vision, as their wings fold closed and they become a sliver on a leaf or flower, or as they dip and disappear into tall grass."

You can see these insects and plants, a number from the Abbey Arboretum, featured throughout *The Saint John's Bible* by artist Chris Tomlin:

Gospels and Acts

Matthew 11	Blue-eyed darner dragonfly (*Aeshna multicolor*)
Matthew 17	Clouded yellow butterfly (*Colias croceus*) Orange sulphur butterfly (*Colias eurytheme*)
Mark 16	Monarch butterfly (*Danaus plexippus*) Milkweed (*Asclepias syriaca*)
Acts 12	Sulphur family butterfly (*Colias eurytheme*)
Acts 20	Peacock butterfly (*Inachis io*)

Pentateuch

Genesis 4	Swallowtail butterfly (*Papilio machaon*) on a milk thistle (*Silybum marianum*)
Genesis 4/5	Swallowtail butterfly (*Papilio machaon*)
Ezekiel 22	Damselflies (*Zygoptera*)

Prophets

Isaiah 30	Scarab beetle (*Scarabaeidae*)
Jeremiah 17	African field crickets (*Gryllus bimaclatus*)
Jeremiah 35	Cicada (*Cicadidae*)
Ezekiel 22	Robber fly (*Asilidae*)

Wisdom Books

Song of Solomon 1	Clouded yellow butterfly (*Colias croceus*)
	Orange sulphur butterfly (*Colias eurytheme*)
Wisdom of Solomon 7	Bumblebee (*Bombus terrestris*)

Historical Books

2 Samuel 24	Army ant workers (*Eciton burchelli*)
	Grasshopper (*Orthoptera caelifera*)
2 Kings 16	Emperor scorpion (*Pandinus imperator*)
	Arizona bark scorpion (*Centruroides sculpturatus*)
1 Chronicles 25	Leafcutter ants (*Acromyrmex* and *Atta*)
2 Chronicles 11	Raingtailed lemur (*Lemur catta*)
2 Chronicles 27	Praying mantis (*Mantis religiosa*)
	Banded demoiselle (*Calopteryx splendens*)
Ezra 1	Harlequin beetle (*Acrocinus longimanus*)
Tobit 14	Wasps (*Hymenoptera apocrita*)
Judith 15	Whip spider (*Amblypygi*) eating Monarch butterfly (*Danaus plexippus*)
1 Maccabees 4	Gold beetle (*Chrysina resplendens*)
	Silver beetle (*Chrysina bates*)
1 Maccabees 11	Glasswing butterfly (*Greta oto*)
	Black widow spider (*Latrodectus mactans*)
2 Maccabees 7	Painted lady butterfly (Vanessa cardui)
	Caterpillars (*Lepidoptera*)
2 Maccabees 15	Chameleon (*Chamaeleonidae*)

Entering Saint John's

It's tempting to rush from the stress of Interstate 94 into the Saint John's Abbey Arboretum. Please observe the speed limit on County Road 159. This slows you down to "Benedictine time" and prepares you for a peaceful visit to a place where nature has its own quiet rhythm and pace. Nothing is rushed in the forest, prairie, or wetlands.

For a Safe Walk

Saint John's is what it is because of where it is. The six trails in this guide have emerged the past century and a half from an intimate union and stewardship between the monastic community of Saint John's Abbey and its sacred landscape. The Abbey keeps its arboretum less humanized or "civilized" to reveal the hand of God. For this reason, there are few trail signs in the arboretum to guide or distract you. Time takes its course in the arboretum, which is why you'll see blown-down trees in the forest. They decay slowly to enrich the soil and serve as wildlife habitat and seedbeds.

If you're not familiar with the Abbey Arboretum trails, it's good to keep yourself oriented with the maps in this field guide and a compass or smart phone compass. When you're on a trail, look behind you every once in a while. This familiarizes you with the terrain and gives you a reverse view of the path, which helps on your return to the trailhead. Note the trail's terrain, which can be smooth, rutted, rocky, or have exposed tree roots. If you're lost or injured on the trails, call Saint John's Life Safety at 320-363-2144.

In the spring, summer, and autumn, it's best to carry mosquito repellent and sun lotion. In spring and summer, watch for wood ticks and deer ticks (*Ixodes scapularis*), which can carry Lyme and other diseases. Wear slacks tucked into socks and light-colored clothing to make it easier to spot ticks. After your hike, check yourself thoroughly for them. If you find a tick on your body, remove it as soon as possible with a tweezers, and disinfect the bite with antiseptic. For more information, please see the websites of the Minnesota Department of Health and the Minnesota Department of Natural Resources.

Leave No Trace

Saint John's Abbey adheres to the "leave no trace" principles of outdoor ethics. Please leave rocks, plants, and other natural objects as you find them. Avoid introducing or transporting nonnative species or disturbing wildlife. If you bring or find trash please take it with you. No unauthorized vehicles are allowed in the Abbey Arboretum, nor are unauthorized fires, motorboats, dogs or pets, trapping, firearms, or weapons. Camping and the harvesting of plants, mushrooms, timber, or wildlife is by permit only. (Mushrooms in central Minnesota can be poisonous. Do not eat any wild mushrooms unless you're absolutely sure of the species.) Bikes are allowed only on paved roads. If you have any questions about the Abbey Arboretum's policies, please call 320-363-2144.

When he established the heavens, I was there,
    when he drew a circle on the face of the deep,
when he made firm the skies above,
    when he established the fountains of the deep,
when he assigned to the sea its limit,
    so that the waters might not transgress his command,
when he marked out the foundations of the earth,
    then I was beside him, like a master worker;
and I was daily his delight,
    rejoicing before him always,
rejoicing in his inhabited world
    and delighting in the human race.

    —Proverbs 8:27-31

Bottom Lands

As we walk beyond the field,
out into the tree laced lip of the marsh,
our feet begin to sink into the sodden land.

We separate to find our own easy path.

You have gone across the high grasses,
beyond these careful edges and out
into the midst of the marsh.

I still skirt the bog trees,
    stumble over exposed roots.
The trunks are dead,
heavy branched but twigless,

stark against the single moon
and the leaves of the living trees.
I am gazing up, open mouthed,

witness to my own subsumption.

In the middle, your feet are soaked
    through your socks.
The trees are wreathed around you.
The night sky gapes above you.

We call out.
    Our voices are muffled, half-heard.

I am saying to you now
that the way these fireflies light up
one after the other,
    and a thousand at the same time,

makes them a living set of stars
gathering around one white and blue moon
which I cannot even see.

—Ryan Kutter, SJU '03

Let ours be a time remembered for the awakening of a new reverence for life, the firm resolve to achieve sustainability, the quickening of the struggle for justice and peace, and the joyful celebration of life.

—*Earth Charter*, The Hague (June 29, 2000), quoted in *Laudato Sì*, no. 207

Father, we praise you with all your creatures.
We came forth from your all-powerful hand;
they are yours, filled with your presence and your
   tender love.
Praise be to you!

—Pope Francis, *Laudato Sì*, A Christian Prayer in Union with Creation

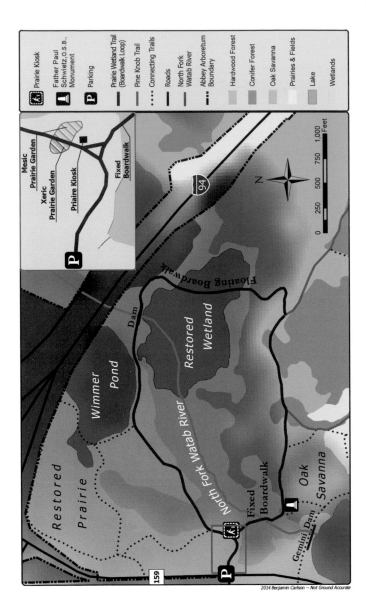

Prairie Kiosk

Father Paul Schwietz, O.S.B., Monument

Parking

Prairie Wetland Trail (Boardwalk Loop)

Pine Knob Trail

Connecting Trails

Roads

North Fork Watab River

Abbey Arboretum Boundary

Hardwood Forest

Conifer Forest

Oak Savanna

Prairies & Fields

Lake

Wetlands

Mesic Prairie Garden

Xeric Prairie Garden

Priaire Kiosk

Fixed Boardwalk

Restored Prairie

Wimmer Pond

Dam

Restored Wetland

Floating Boardwalk

North Fork Watab River

Fixed Boardwalk

Oak Savanna

Gemini Dam

N

0   250   500   750   1,000
Feet

2014 Benjamin Carlson -- Not Ground Accurate

Prairie-Wetlands Trail

1.5-mile loop • 45–60 minutes

Awareness of God: To look for God not in the abstract but in the ordinary events of every day. "We believe that the divine presence is everywhere" (RB 19).

The Trail

The trail begins at the kiosk just east of County Road 159 (please see map). School buses are here often. This trail is popular for field trips, offering children and their teachers a convenient way to experience a diversity of landscape and wetland.

Heading south from the kiosk the trail crosses a short boardwalk, flanked by two tall tamarack trees (*Larix laricina*). They were planted in 2002 by John Geissler, who headed the Arboretum after the death of Father Paul Schwietz, O.S.B.

The boardwalk passes over the North Fork of the Watab River (you may hear it gurgling in

spring, summer, and fall), hidden in cattails. The trail goes left, past the edge of the oak savanna on the right, and up a wide, grassy path. The trail turns left through a grove of tall pines and spruce onto a pine-rimmed logging road, past a stand of birch, through tall pines on the right and hardwood forest on the left. About a half mile into the walk the trail goes left onto a smaller path that curves downhill northward. The trail shortly becomes cinder (to prevent erosion and rutting) as it approaches the long boardwalk over the restored wetlands, through tall cattails as the boardwalk widens into trapezoids.

The Minnesota Department of Natural Resources (DNR) helped create this shallow wetland by funding a dam on the North Fork of the Watab River in 1988. The dam mimics natural changes by raising the flow of the river through the wetlands in the spring, drowning nonnative plants and helping waterfowl feed, and lowers it in July and August, allowing plants to seed and exposing mud flats for shorebirds. Shallow wetlands are habitat for ducks and geese, and shorebirds, including over fifty solitary sandpipers who, on July 31, 2006, chose not to be solitary and gathered in the wetlands where they were observed by Dr. Phil Chu of the biology department, an ornithologist. A pair of mudhens, common in Florida but rare in Minnesota, have raised broods here. A pair of trumpeter swans began raising a family here in 2010. Some 21 million shorebirds of some forty species fly north every spring; perhaps a million of them move through Minnesota.

At the end of the boardwalk the trail enters a small grove of tall pines and prairie grass and joins a dirt road over the North Fork of the Watab River, flowing north under Interstate 94. The trail passes through another grove of tall pines and over the dam that created the restored wetland and Wimmer Pond, named after Abbot Boniface Wimmer, O.S.B. (1809–1887), founder of the first Benedictine monastery in the United States, at Latrobe, Pennsylvania.

Heading back south toward the kiosk the trail passes through Father Paul Schwietz's restored prairie with its native plants.* One of them, the big bluestem, can have roots ten feet deep (three times longer than the plant itself). This enables them to absorb even small amounts of water from the soil. Bluestem once covered thousands of miles of Minnesota prairie, ninety percent of which now is farmland. "If you are fortunate and the wind is just right," wrote Ron Wienhold, who walks this trail often, "you can listen as the grasses make their own music with the rubbing of stems and leaves . . . with the blowing of snow crystals, it becomes a quiet symphony of winter on the prairie."

> Holy, holy, holy is the LORD of hosts;
> the whole earth is full of his glory.
>
> —Isaiah 6:3

* Such as big bluestem, purple prairie clover, alum root, slender penstemon, golden aster, prairie onion, white prairie clover, porcupine grass, prairie smoke, Missouri goldenrod, little bluestem, pasque flower, prairie dropseed, long-leaved bluets, round-headed bush clover, stiff sunflower, yarrow, and prairie phlox.

Prairie-Wetlands Vegetation

Big bluestem *Andropogon gerardii*
- *Late Summer–Autumn*

Grows three to six feet tall in tufted bunches or turfs. Stems are often purplish or bluish, topped with three to four blooms that resemble turkey tracks, giving rise to another common name: Turkey-foot grass. Leaves turn reddish bronze after a frost.

Notable: *Andropogon*, from the Greek *andros* (man) and *pogon* (beard), refers to the hairy spikelets of this genus that look like a man's beard.

At Saint John's
Ellory Eggermont Roske, CSB '11, chose it for its strength, abundance, and beauty as a component of a signature paper she made by hand for the College of Saint Benedict, supporting the Benedictine value of environmental sustainability.

Little bluestem *Schizachyrium scoparium*
- *Late Summer–Autumn*

Grows in dense bunches or clusters up to four feet tall. Flowers near the top of stalks have long, white hairs giving a feathery appearance. Leaves turn bronze or dark orange after frost.

Notable: Birds such as the prairie chicken or sharp-tailed grouse eat its seeds.

At Saint John's

Makes up much of the grass in the Abbey Arboretum's restored prairie.

Sideoats grama *Bouteloua curtipendula*
- *Midsummer–Autumn*

Short, densely flowered, comb-like flowering heads hang to one side of the stem like a feathered lance. Is one of the dominant grasses of the prairie, especially in drier areas; native from southern Canada through Mexico and Central America into western South America.

Notable: Kiowa warriors who had killed an enemy with a lance often wore a dried stem of sideoats as a decoration.

At Saint John's

An easy prairie grass to germinate and grow; Outdoor U often sells it at the annual spring plant sale in May.

Butterflyweed *Asclepias tuberosa* • *Summer*

Grows rapidly to one to three feet tall, somewhat sprawling or bushy. Branched flower clusters are relatively flat with up to twenty-five flowers per cluster. Most often brilliant orange but can vary from yellow to red. Unlike other milkweeds, this species has clear rather than milky sap.

Notable: *Asclepias* was the Greek god of healing; Swedish botanist Carl Linnaeus (1707–1778), father of modern taxonomy, chose the genus name for milkweeds because of their many medicinal uses.

At Saint John's

One evening out by the prairie kiosk, a monk interrupted a person digging up a blooming butterflyweed to transplant to his home. When asked why he was stealing a plant, the would-be gardener, Adam-like, said his wife made him do it. He didn't know that the deep taproot of the butterflyweed, when the plant is old enough to bloom, makes it nearly impossible to transplant successfully.

Pasque flower *Pulsatilla patens*
- *Early Spring*

Low, delicate plants emerge shortly after snow melts. Pale white to lavender or purple flowers on each stem have five to eight petal-like sepals (modified leaves that encase the developing flower) surrounding a bright yellow center. The plant is covered in soft, spreading hairs.

Notable: One of the earliest plants to bloom in Minnesota, "Pasque" refers to its bloom time in the Easter or Paschal season.

At Saint John's

These early flowers are a welcome sight around the kiosk as grade-school students explore the prairie in spring classes.

Purple coneflower *Echinacea angustifolia* and
Echinacea purpurea • *Summer*

Grows two to four feet tall and three to eight inches long, with rough leaves and a prickly stem. Purple petals droop from a cone-shaped flower head and can be up to three inches long. *E. purpurea* has wider leaves with rounder bases.

Notable: Once used by Native Americans to treat a variety of ailments, including toothaches, *Echinacea* is still commonly used as an herbal remedy today.

At Saint John's

Outdoor U naturalists review coneflower species every summer.

E. angustifolia is the only purple coneflower species native to Minnesota and is common at Saint John's. *E. angustifolia* and *E. purpurea* can be difficult to distinguish, especially since they readily hybridize. *E. purpurea* is a common garden cultivar, often found in restoration seed mixes.

Black-eyed Susan *Rudbeckia hirta*

• *Summer*

Bright yellow, two- to three-inch-wide daisy-like flowers with dark centers grow singly on stems one to three feet tall. The stems and scattered oval leaves are coarse, covered with bristly hairs. A common and highly visible flower in prairies, fields, and roadside ditches.

Notable: Native across much of the United States and Canada and can behave as an annual, biennial, or short-lived perennial, depending on the climate and growing conditions.

At Saint John's

Black-eyed Susans are relatively easy to propagate from seed, a vibrant addition to restored prairies or native flower gardens. You can often find them at the annual Outdoor U plant sale.

Duckweed *Lemnaceae* • *Summer*

Small floating plants, a fifth of an inch in diameter. Plants are tiny, with one to six short roots. Duckweeds sometimes produce microscopic flowers but primarily depend on vegetative division for reproduction. Grows in green blankets on ponds, swamps, or marshes.

Notable: Floating carpets of duckweed camouflage frogs and small turtles. Geese, ducks, and muskrats depend on duckweed as a major food source, often ninety percent of their diet.

At Saint John's

"What's all that green stuff?" is a common refrain (and an apt description of duckweed) from preK–12 youth as they cross the boardwalk on Outdoor U field trips.

Cattails *Typha latifolia* • *Spring–Autumn*

Perennial herb, grows to nine feet tall along shorelines and in shallow water with broad, ribbon-like leaves. The familiar brown "cats' tails" have thousands of tiny flowers packed densely into cylindrical spikes. In late fall and winter, the spikes expand and the wind disperses the seed in fluffy clumps.

Notable: These familiar plants provide shelter for songbirds and waterfowl and food for muskrats. Roots, shoots, and stems are all edible. Even the pollen can be used as a flour substitute. Wild edible enthusiast Euell Gibbons (1911–1975) called cattails the "swamp supermarket."

At Saint John's

You will also see *T. angustifolia*, an invasive European species. Its leaves are narrower than our native variety, but the two species hybridize.

Tamarack *Larix laricina* • *Summer green; Autumn yellow*

Slender, cone-bearing tree, grows up to eighty-five feet tall in wetlands and in open areas in full sun. Leaves are short, soft needles and grow in tufts on branches. In autumn, the needles turn bright golden yellow and fall, making tamarack the only deciduous conifer in Minnesota.

Notable: Tamarack is fast growing (up to six inches per year) and resists decay. The Ojibwe stripped the roots of tamarack into sturdy threads for sewing birch bark canoes.

At Saint John's

Two tamaracks flank the fixed boardwalk near the prairie kiosk. The original 1860s homestead at Saint John's, near the current Lake Wobegon Trail, was built from tamarack.

Tickseed *Coreopsis palmata* • *Summer*

Grows one to two feet tall on a slender, erect stem topped with showy yellow ray flowers. Underground rhizomes spread and form a dense mat that can help stabilize dry, sandy soils. Also called "Bird's foot coreopsis" due to its distinct three-pronged leaves that resemble a bird's foot.

Notable: Some American Indians believed topical application of the seeds on affected areas would alleviate pain from ailments such as rheumatism.

At Saint John's
Outdoor U staff sometimes call this flower "crow-eopsis," a pneumonic device to remember the plant name by the distinctive shape of its leaves.

Blazing star *Liatris sp.*   •   *Late Summer–Autumn*

There are five species of blazing star in Minnesota. They're known for their flower heads in dense clusters in shades of purple. The stems, growing two to five feet tall, are covered with slender, grass-like leaves. Botanists distinguish the different species of this flower by comparing their "bracts," unique for each species. A bract is a modified or specialized leaf, often part of a flower's reproductive system.

Notable: Unusual among flowers, blazing stars bloom from top to bottom.

At Saint John's
Prairie blazing star (*L. pycnostachya*) and dotted blazing star (*L. punctata*) are similar species in the Abbey Arboretum. Rough blazing star (*L. aspera*) flower clusters are more "button" than "spike shaped."

Prairie-Wetlands Wildlife

Skippers *Lepidoptera; Family Hesperiidae*
- *Late Spring–Autumn*

Small, robust butterflies characteristic of prairie ecosystems. Most are grass feeders. Adults pollinate a variety of native flower species. Antennae are widely separated and the tips usually curve inward. Skippers hold their front and hind wings at different angles when at rest. Several species are common on the prairie.

   Notable: Nine varieties of skippers are on the Minnesota list of endangered, threatened, and "special concern" species. "Skipper" refers to their rapid, erratic flight pattern.

At Saint John's
Skippers overwinter as larvae or pupae in the base of grasses, so they're vulnerable during prairie burns. Saint John's follows a prairie burn cycle, burning only parts of the prairie each year to help maintain healthy populations of these and other prairie species.

Dragonflies/nymphs
Odonata • *Summer*

Dragonflies spend most of their life in the water. Some exist as nymphs in the water for several years before emerging as adults for just a few months. Nymphs

are jet propelled, drawing water through the gills at the rectum and expelling it.

Notable: Dragonflies are distinguished from damselflies by their strong build, flat wings when perched, and connected eyes. Damselflies have a slender build, hold their wings over their backs when perched, and have separate eyes. Dragonflies are carnivorous, feeding on insects.

At Saint John's
Biology professor Dr. James Poff calls the transformation of the dragonfly from aquatic nymph to an insect with iridescent blue and green wings "one of the miracles of the biological world."

Water boatman *Corixidae* • *Summer*

Small, oval-shaped aquatic insect; less than a half-inch long. Hind legs are long and serve as oars to help the boatman swim rapidly. Feeds on algae and microscopic aquatic organisms; common in lakes, ponds, and streams.

Notable: Water boatmen are dark but can appear silvery due to the envelope of air that serves as its oxygen supply. This air makes it difficult for the insect to stay underwater so it grabs onto plants and other objects to stay submerged.

At Saint John's
Water boatmen are among the most mesmerizing and exciting insects for youth to find and learn about in the wetland, especially when dipping for macroinvertebrates on preK–12 field trips.

Plains pocket gopher *Geomys bursarius* • *Year-round*

Medium-sized gopher, grows up to thirteen inches long. Brown coat with a large body, short legs, small eyes, and ears. It's named for the large external, fur-lined pouches in its cheeks that it uses to collect and transport food to its burrow system. Digs underground tunnels; rarely seen above ground.

Notable: Gophers control the "thermostat" and humidity of their burrows by plugging entry holes with dirt. Their lips are close behind their incisors, allowing them to dig with their teeth, as well as their feet, without getting soil in their mouths.

At Saint John's

The gophers' tunnels (marked by sandy mounds throughout the prairie) benefit the environment by aerating the soil, filtering water, and reducing soil compaction. Badgers often move into the prairie and dig out the gophers when the gophers become abundant.

Beaver *Castor canadensis* • *Year-round*

Largest rodent in North America, weighing forty to sixty-five pounds. The beaver's broad, flat, scaly tail is a rudder for steering when swimming, a tripod for balance when cutting trees, and a warning signal when slapped against the water to alarm predators. Beavers change the landscape more dramatically than any other animal, except humans,

by cutting down trees, damming streams, and building lodges in ponds and wetlands.

Notable: For nearly two hundred years beaver felt hats were the highest fashion statement; demand for them in Europe nearly exhausted the North American population through the fur trade. Beavers have repopulated and are common in wetlands, especially near aspen.

At Saint John's

Beavers often plug culverts to save work on dam building, such as on the south end of Stumpf Lake. Saint John's uses a "Clemson leveler," a pipe that extends through the culvert and thirty feet upstream, to prevent beavers from hearing the rushing water, so they dam the culvert but don't plug the upstream intake.

> And God said, "Let the earth bring forth living creatures of every kind: cattle and creeping things and wild animals of the earth of every kind." And it was so. God made the wild animals of the earth of every kind, and the cattle of every kind, and everything that creeps upon the ground of every kind. And God saw that it was good.
>
> —Genesis 1:24-25

Tiger salamander *Ambystoma tigrinum*
- *Early Spring–Autumn*

Largest land salamander in Minnesota, about seven to thirteen inches long. They are dark green to black with yellow spots and a light-colored belly. Spends much of the year underground but emerges if the soil becomes too saturated. The salamander's slimy skin, an important defense mechanism, can cause irritation in humans, especially to the eyes.

Notable: This carnivorous salamander has a diverse diet and is even known to eat its own larvae. The sign of a cannibal morph adult is quite clear: these salamanders grow much larger heads than their counterparts.

At Saint John's

Tiger salamanders are large and fairly common in a variety of habitats across Minnesota but we find the smaller blue-spotted salamander (three to five inches long) much more often in the Abbey Arboretum.

Trumpeter swan *Cygnus buccinator*

- *Spring–Autumn*

Huge waterfowl, larger than geese; fifty-four to sixty inches long, eighty-inch wingspan. Long neck, all white body, and black bill. No visible distinction between male and female. The trumpeter swan is named for its deep, nasal, trumpeting call. Found in lakes, ponds, large rivers.

Notable: Excessive hunting for its feathers in the 1600s–1800s caused a significant decline in numbers. Its largest flight feathers were made into what were considered the highest quality quill pens.

At Saint John's

In 2012 a pair of trumpeter swans was seen in the Abbey Arboretum wetlands with three cygnets (baby swans), the first time baby swans had been in the Arboretum in about one hundred years.

Great blue heron *Ardea herodias* • *Spring–Autumn*

Large, leggy, long-necked wading bird common near shores of open water in wetlands across North America, Central America, the Caribbean, and the Galapagos Islands. Six species of heron live in Minnesota in spring and summer: great blue heron, black-crowned night heron, green heron, great egret, American bittern, and least bittern.

Notable: Largest of North America's twelve heron species, about four feet tall, often chooses highest treetops for nests, feeds mostly on nongame fish, aquatic insects, crayfish, frogs, and mice. Often swallow their food alive, sometimes catching a fish and flipping it into the air so it goes down headfirst.

At Saint John's

This photo was voted "Best in Show" in the first Outdoor U photo contest (2007). At the time, Liam Cofell Dwyer was a student at Saint John's Prep, winning against several seasoned photographers. Herons were plentiful at Saint John's when there was a great blue heron rookery along the Sauk River between Cold Spring and Rockville. Biology professor Dr. Nick Zaczkowski regularly took students to visit the rookery in the 1970s and 1980s. For unknown reasons, the herons abandoned the rookery in 1989.

Wetlands Floating Boardwalk

In the winter of 2000 several hundred volunteers dragged sections of 1,350 feet of boardwalk onto the ice and installed them over the Abbey Arboretum wetlands, between County

Road 159 and Interstate 94. The board-walk, first envisioned by Father Paul Schwietz, O.S.B., lets you see this ecosystem firsthand, from prairie grass through the wetlands up into the rolling hills of the savanna. In the summer you can see hundreds of leopard and mink frogs leaping ahead of you, with a "knock-knock-knock" call that sounds like a carpenter at work. On the wetlands' surface, in the green vegetation known as duckweed, you can spot dragonfly nymphs, back-swimmers, snails, and predaceous diving

beetles. The boardwalk connects to the deciduous forest bordering the restored habitat and into the century-old pine plantation. For school children the boardwalk can be a hobbit-like journey. As one third grader, Spencer, wrote in 2006, "We made it safely across the bridge of doom! Now we are entering . . . let me think—now we are entering the land of eternal thirst!"

The Prairie Garden

The prairie garden near the kiosk has dozens of species of labeled native plants to help you identify those you may see on your walk, including the dry (xeric) species on the top of the hill and the wetter (mesic) species at the bottom of the hill. By 2000, this restored prairie had more than half the species present in local prairies in 1900 and some 80 percent that were present in 1950. At

first glance, compared to wetland and forest, the prairie looks monochromatic, but if one pauses and looks closer, wrote Emily Reimer, CSB '14, there are "eclectic bursts of bright colors of the prairie flowers" and the prairie grasses shed pods and seeds of all colors.

Habitat Restoration Project

You send forth your spirit; they are created, and you renew the face of the earth. —Psalm 104:30

By the mid-twentieth century the monastic community and its growing university and prep school had become too large to farm self-sufficiently. In 1986, Father Paul Schwietz, O.S.B., with Michael Maurer and Fred Bengston of the Minnesota Department of Natural Resources, conceived of converting the former cow pasture to wetlands, savanna, and prairie. Two years later, volunteers built two earth dams to hold back water for sixty acres of wetlands. Then they resurrected the fields into a brilliant ecosystem of over ninety species of native grasses and flowers. The restored savanna, prairie, and wetlands are now a small prairie ecosystem of about 150 acres.

When the Benedictines arrived in the 1860s the closest prairies were in Saint Joseph and Avon. The monks cleared this forested area for farming. The landscape remained that way until the 1990s when Father Paul created a prairie here by hiring a bulldozer to shape the flat fields into wetland depressions and contoured uplands. The operator of the bulldozer was uncertain about what contour to create until Father Paul advised, "Just build it like *God* would have built it."

Restoring Habitat with Fire

Every spring and fall, Saint John's restores and protects the prairie habitat with "prescribed burns." This prompts the growth of native prairie plants (whose roots go down as much as fifteen feet), releases nutrients from dead plants into the soil, and suppresses invasive species and woody vegetation. These prescribed burns, the first in 1986, mimic the natural fires once started by lightning or by Native Americans for hunting habitat. Oak savannas—prairies scattered with bur oak trees (resilient to fire because of their thick bark)—are transition zones between the prairie and hardwood forests (oak, maple, basswood, elm) that need to be protected with fire. Student-volunteer Adam Halbur, SJU '98, described one such burn in April 1998: "With a west wind, a back burn was started on the downwind side, the eastern side of the prairie along Wimmer Pond. Once secured, crews started burning the northern and southern sides. The firebreaks were wetted to keep the fire from jumping. Then the two torchers walked toward each other along the western side. In a gush of wind, the prairie was ashes in a few minutes."

Saint John's Birdman

A young monk and new priest, Lambert Thelen, O.S.B., was one of the first to document bird life at Saint John's. Born in Chicago in 1874, he moved with his parents to Saint Michael, Minnesota, graduated from Saint John's in 1894, professed his monastic vows, and joined the college faculty as a professor and prefect. He was, said one confrere, "gifted with a serious and steady character . . . always kind and cheerful." With pencil and pad, preserved today in the Abbey archives, he made frequent notes on birds during his walks through woods, prairie, and wetlands of Saint John's, recording the movement of chickadees, orioles, woodpeckers, swallows, bobolinks, shrikes, larks, martins, blue jays, owls, hawks, and scarlet tanagers. "Yesterday a nest of Prairie Horned Larks, containing two eggs, was reported to me," he wrote on April 4, 1895, "and I was surprised to find two baby birds in it." In 1898 he developed symptoms of what later was diagnosed as tuberculosis. He was sent to Colorado "to find relief in the air

of the mountain region." He died March 8, 1900, and his body was returned to Saint John's for burial in the Abbey cemetery. He was twenty-six.

Happy are those who sing with all their heart,
    from the bottoms of their hearts.
To find joy in the sky, the trees, the flowers.
There are always flowers for those who want to see them.

    —Henri Matisse, *Jazz*

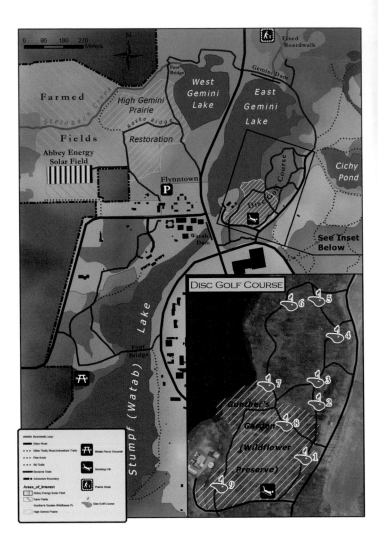

Savanna-Prairie Trail

1-mile loop   •   **20–30 minutes**

Dignity of Work: To appreciate the dignity of work in God's creation. "They live by the labor of their hands" (RB 48).

The Trail

The trail begins at the kiosk and has wide, smooth paths of mowed grass and dirt, and a dirt road. It's a comfortable walk with gentle slopes and rolling hills of savanna with tall, husky bur oaks and white oaks, restored prairie grass, and wild flowers. Tucked discreetly into the savanna is a nine-hole disc golf course, fostered and maintained by Saint John's students. The course, with marble slabs and chain baskets for each hole, is mowed in the summer and an easy way to tour the savanna and prairie. The trail also includes a snow-sledding hill and a rope swing on one of the huge oaks, an ideal viewing spot for the savanna, prairie, and wetlands.

This trail begins at the same starting point as the Prairie-Wetlands. From the kiosk, walk south between two tall tamarack

trees onto the three hundred-foot-long fixed boardwalk, through cattails and over the North Fork of the Watab River.

At the end of the fixed boardwalk, veer right onto a dirt path that rises to a hill with a large boulder with a plaque honoring Father Paul Schwietz, O.S.B. This hill offers an excellent northward vista of the boardwalk loop and the prairie wetlands. Follow the grassy path south where, in autumn, one can see to the right a large field of prairie sage (*Artemisia ludoviciana*).

Proceed right at a split in the grassy path and take the dirt road left (east), with East Gemini Lake on your right. Go east

on this dirt road, into a denser savanna of oak forest. A wide-mowed path on the right is a brief diversion to a peninsula with a view of East Gemini and County Road 159. Return to the dirt road and up a sloping hill, with the radio tower visible to the south. Bear right at a tall mound at the top of the hill.

Soon to the right, just before a beautiful stand of quaking aspen (*Populus tremuloides*) that flame yellow in the autumn, there's an unmarked, grassy path (photo, next page). This path passes down through the quaking aspen, as if through a rabbit hole, and up a small hill to a concrete and wood bench with an elevated view of East Gemini Lake to the north. Follow the trail south to

basket no. 7 with another stand of quaking aspen on the left and the lake on the right. After the tee for hole no. 8, there's a post sign for "wild flower reserve #72" bordering the lake. At the juncture in the disc golf path go right to a high point above the lake. The trail goes south, with the water treatment plant on the right and the snow-sledding hill visible in the distance to the left. The trail comes to the top of the hill. Turn left on the dirt road, just north across the asphalt road from Warner Palaestra, visible through the woods on the right. The dirt road rises to a sloping hill with the university baseball fields visible on the right, a hilltop view of the sledding hill with East Gemini Lake to the north, and County Road 159 winding along its western shore. Down the hill a wide grassy path slopes north into an oak forest northward and uphill back toward the view of East Gemini Lake. The trail returns to the grassy path, goes left onto the dirt road, back to the Paul Schwietz boulder, across the fixed boardwalk, and back to the kiosk.

> The land isn't merely a buffer to the outside world, but a physical manifestation of the beauty of creation. It is a way for resources to be used to proclaim a Gospel value— that all creation is good.
>
> —Paul Schwietz, O.S.B.

Vegetation of the Savanna-Prairie

Bur oak *Quercus macrocarpa* • *Year-round*

Large hardwood tree, grows to 110 feet tall. Bark is gray with thick ridges and deep furrows. Leaves have rounded lobes with velvety undersides. The tips of the leaves are wider than the base of the leaf compared to white oaks. Acorns have large caps with fringed margins.

Notable: The Latin for oak, *Quercus*, means "beautiful tree." The thick bark of the bur oak makes it a suitable savanna species, well adapted for fire tolerance. Bur oaks are the most common oak in Minnesota.

At Saint John's

Bur oak (with northern pin oak) are the least common native oaks at Saint John's, but you can see many of them in the oak savanna.

Purple prairie-clover *Dalea purpurea* • *Summer*

Perennial, eight to thirty-five inches tall. It's an herbaceous plant (leaves and stems die down to the soil at the end of the growing season) but its stem is woody. Bright purple flowers at the top of the plant are in dense, cylindrical spikes, one to two inches long.

Notable: True clovers (genus *Trifolium*) are invasive; prairie-clovers (*Dalea*) are part of the legume family of beans and peas native to North America. Purple prairie-clover has stout taproots that can be six feet deep.

At Saint John's
The Abbey Arboretum's other native true clover is *Dalea candida* (white prairie clover), similar to *D. Purpurea* but with (surprise!) white flowers.

Hoary alyssum *Berteroa incana* • *Summer*

Tiny white flowers with four deeply divided petals clustered along an erect branched hairy, or "hoary," stem. Grows eighteen to twenty-four inches tall; most abundant in disturbed dry areas, fields, and dry prairies where vegetation is sparse. A member of the mustard family (*Brassicaceae*), it emerges early in spring and produces flowers from June until frost.

Notable: *B. incana* is an invasive species, native to Europe. Because of an old belief that they cured rabies, alyssums have also been called madwort or heal-bite.

At Saint John's
When Outdoor U staff were teaching in the prairie, one student misheard the name of this plant as "horny asylum," which turns out to be an apt pneumonic device to help remember this plant.

Leadplant *Amorpha canescens* • *Summer*

Perennial plant, one to three feet tall. Has several tiny, grayish green leaflets. Flowers are small and purple, with long, bright yellow anthers (pollen-producing structures). This shrub has

deep roots; difficult to transplant. Also found in open woodlands with direct sun.

Notable: Some mining prospectors and farmers in the late nineteenth and early twentieth century believed it grew over lead deposits (since proven false), a possible source of its name.

At Saint John's

Leadplant is fire resistant and drought resistant, hardy enough to be one of the only shrubs in our prairie. We've been told that a sign of a mature prairie is the presence of a healthy leadplant population.

Gray-headed coneflower *Ratibida pinnata* • *Summer*

Flowers are composite (daisy-like); disk flowers are green-gray and turn brown; ray flowers (look like petals) are long and yellow and point downward like a typical coneflower. Grows up to four feet tall with hairy, rigid stems. Leaves are five to eight inches long.

Notable: A common look-alike is prairie coneflower (*Ratibida columnifera*), which has a more elongated (column-like) head than the gray-headed coneflower, with petals often marked with red.

At Saint John's

You'll often see this flower growing along the trail near the prairie kiosk. The Outdoor U sensory class for preschool and kindergarten encourages children to crush the mature seed heads in the fall to smell the strong anise or citrus scent before scattering the seeds in the prairie.

Prickly ash *Zanthoxylum americanum* • *Year-round*

Upright shrub, grows to twenty feet tall. Gray to brown branches, bare spines a third of an inch long. Leaves are compound, with five to thirteen leaflets. In summer, red fruits mature in clusters and give off a citrusy fragrance (*not* edible). Thrives in open areas and forms thickets.

Notable: Despite its name, prickly ash is not related to true ash trees. The inner bark has a citrus smell and the fruits have numbing qualities, once said to relieve toothaches.

At Saint John's

While playing a hide-and-seek game called "Thicket" to practice their camouflage and observation skills, preK–12 students on Outdoor U field trips quickly learn to use caution when they find themselves hiding in a thicket of prickly ash.

Absinthe wormwood *Artemisia absinthium* • *Summer*

Perennial herbaceous plant, one to three feet tall, begins blooming in Minnesota in mid-July. Gray-green leaves with fine, soft hairs. Grows in dry soil with a deep, woody taproot; thrives in the prairie and along roadsides. Similar in color to the native prairie sage, though leaf shapes are distinct.

Notable: Native to Eurasia and is now established across much of the United States. The plant was introduced to the United States for medicinal purposes to aid digestion; traditional ingredient for making absinthe.

People either love or hate the smell of this plant, making wormwood another Outdoor U field trip favorite when students crush up the leaves and cast their votes. Word of warning: wash your hands after handling this plant, the votes are pretty much unanimous on how it tastes.

Common milkweed *Asclepias syriaca* • *Summer*

Grows three to five feet tall with long, oval-shaped leaves attached to the stem in pairs. Dusty purple flowers grow in a domed, droopy cluster at the top of the plant. Milkweeds have spiky, fuzzy seedpods that grow three to four inches long. Inside each pod are hundreds of seeds, each with a white tuft that disperses with the wind.

Notable: Milkweed's milky sap contains cardiac glycosides, making it toxic to mammals. Some insects, like the monarch butterfly, are immune to the sap and eat the bitter chemicals to protect themselves from predators. Monarchs complete their lifecycle on milkweed plants.

At Saint John's
Milkweed flowers are edible. A former Outdoor U educator enjoyed adding them to her pancake batter for a bit of pizzazz.

Goldenrod *Solidago sp.* • *Late Summer*

Grows up to three feet tall, generally in thickets. Leaves alternate up stem, smallest leaves at the top. Clusters of small yellow or golden flowers. Depending on the species, can be found in the drier part of the prairie, often in disturbed areas, also thrives in moist soil.

Notable: Often known for its healing powers, this plant's genus name *Solidago* is from the Latin *soldare*, "to make whole." Goldenrods are often blamed for seasonal allergies, but since their pollen is not airborne, other plants blooming at the same time (i.e., ragweed) are the real culprits.

At Saint John's

Every year, introductory biology lab students do field work in the Abbey Arboretum, studying how other species interact with goldenrod (see goldenrod gall flies, p. 50).

Jewelweed *Impatiens capensis* • *Late Summer*

Annual wildflower grows to five feet, sign of wet habitat. Smooth, translucent green stems with toothed, egg-shaped leaves. Flowers are bright orange-yellow with brown spots. Fruits are tiny, inflated green pods.

Notable: Another name for jewelweed is spotted touch-me-not. Mature seedpods explode when touched, sending the seeds flying in all directions.

At Saint John's

An Outdoor U science unit on *biomimicry* helps youth identify traits in nature that can be mimicked to solve human problems. The name "jewelweed" refers to the shimmering leaves when silvery water droplets form on its leaves, a trait engineers have tried to imitate in developing self-cleaning windows and paints.

Wildlife of the Savanna-Prairie

Goldenrod gall fly *Eurosta solidaginis* • *Year-round*

Small, brown, winged insect, a fifth of an inch long. Adult female gall flies deposit their eggs into the stem of the goldenrod plant. Eggs hatch in about ten days, and the larva eats the stem as it develops through the winter. In spring, the larva becomes a pupa and then an adult. Adult goldenrod gall flies do not eat, and live about two weeks.

Notable: A chemical in the saliva of the larva causes a reaction in the goldenrod, and a "gall" or ball shape develops around the larva. This becomes a source of food and a place for the larva to live. Downy woodpeckers will break open some galls to eat the larva.

At Saint John's

"On special occasions, my father would take me and my siblings for a drive out to the Saint John's woods," wrote Brian Brown, SJU '89, who was impressed when his father "grasped a goldenrod gall, sliced it open and exposed a maggot nestled inside. Another lesson revealed about adaptation and survival, first taught to my father by my great-grandfather."

Golden orb-weaver *Argiope aurantia* • *Late Summer*

Possibly the largest web-building spider in the northern United States, the adult female body is three-fourths to an inch-and-a-half long. The abdomen is black with two or three pairs of yellow spots in the middle. Webs are flat, circular, up to two or more feet in diameter, decorated with a pair of conspicuous zigzag, vertical lines above and below the web center. Often seen in gardens, fields, and roadsides.

Notable: Known for their ornate webs; harmless to humans. The famous spider from the book *Charlotte's Web* by E. B. White was a barn orb weaver spider (*Araneus cavaticus*) whose full name was given as Charlotte A. Cavatica, referring to her species name.

At Saint John's

Not to be mistaken with the golden silk orb-weaver spider (*Nephila clavipes*), found in warmer climates and not in the Abbey Arboretum.

Grasshoppers *Caelifera* • *Late Summer–Autumn*

Medium-sized insect with large legs, modified for jumping; one to three inches long. Varies from green to yellow to brown. Antennae shorter than body. The "ear" of a grasshopper (called tympanum) is on the abdomen.

Notable: Like humans, grasshoppers are diurnal (active during the day). Crickets are related to grasshoppers but are nocturnal.

At Saint John's

History professor Annette Atkins wrote about the grasshopper plagues in Minnesota in the mid-1870s in her book *Harvest of Grief: Grasshopper Plagues and Public Assistance in Minnesota, 1873–78* (Saint Paul: Minnesota Historical Society), 1984.

Regal fritillary *Speyeria idalia* • *Summer*

One of the most striking butterflies of the temperate regions of North America. Reddish-orange with black forewings and blue-black hind wings. Almost as large as the common monarch butterfly. Breeds only in native prairie habitats.

Notable: The population has declined dramatically in the eastern half of its historical range, vanishing from Michigan, Ohio, Kentucky, and east to the coast. A species of "special concern" in Minnesota (widespread in the west, found in only a few locations in the east).

At Saint John's
Look for adults feeding on nectar of purple coneflower, milkweeds, thistles, and especially blazing stars.

Coyote *Canis latrans*

The coyote is the most abundant large predator in Minnesota. It resembles a small, lean German shepherd with a shaggy grayish coat, large bushy tail, and long, erect ears.

Notable: Diet is diverse, ranging from watermelons to mice and rabbits, and even porcupines. Minnesota DNR researchers believe coyotes kill porcupines by flipping them over and grabbing their throats (not without painful consequences).

At Saint John's
Eleanor Gray, CSB '13, recounts some of the fascinating myths about the "trickster" coyote in the Summer 2011 *Sagatagan Seasons* (online).

Striped skunk *Mephitis mephitis* • *Spring–Autumn*

Medium-sized mammal, about the size of an average house cat, with a glossy black coat and a thin white stripe between its eyes and two stripes on its back. Thrives in country and city. Their distinctive, foul smell helps them avoid most predators, but owls and other birds of prey with a poor sense of smell are unfazed by the odor.

Notable: A good reason to avoid skunks (besides the smell): rabies are more common in striped skunks than in any other Minnesota mammal.

At Saint John's

Skunks generally avoid heavily wooded areas so are most likely to be found on the edges of the Abbey Arboretum, in the prairie, and in semiwooded or open fields.

Prairie skink *Plestiodon septentrionalis* • *Summer–Autumn*

Medium-sized lizard (about five to nine inches long) with short legs and a long tail. Tan, black, and white stripes along the back from head to tail. Males show bright orange chins, throats, and lips during breeding season. Hatchlings have yellow stripes and a bright blue tail. Prairie skinks winter in burrows underground.

Notable: The tail of the prairie skink readily detaches to baffle predators when disturbed. Predators include hawks, owls, raccoons, and shrikes.

At Saint John's
A common lizard in the Abbey Arboretum, found in oak savannas, along stream banks, and in grasslands.

O sing to the LORD a new song;
  Sing to the LORD, all the earth.
Sing to the LORD, bless his name.

—Psalm 96:1-2

Blue jay *Cyanocitta cristata* • *Year-round*

Larger than a robin, smaller than a crow;
eleven inches long. Distinguished by a
bright blue crest on its head. Vibrant blue
to gray, with black and white markings
on wings and tail. A bold, black necklace contrasts the white-gray underside.
Relatives of the crow and raven, blue
jays are intelligent, social birds.

Notable: Feathers appear blue be-
cause of their intricate structures that reflect and refract light,
giving the appearance of blue. A crushed blue jay feather no
longer appears blue (while the red feathers of a cardinal contain a chemical pigment, thus remaining red).

At Saint John's
During Outdoor U field trips students study seed propagation
by pretending to be either blue jays or grey squirrels hiding
and stealing acorns from each other. They make the connection between plant and animal interactions in their habitat

by learning how blue jays help plant trees when they forget a hidden acorn.

Canada goose *Branta Canadensis* • *Spring–Fall*

Large waterfowl, smaller than a swan and larger than a duck, thirty to forty-one inches long; wingspan of four- to five-and-a-half feet. Most common goose in North America. Black head and neck with pale breast and white chin strap. Travel in flocks, flying in V formation. Call is a loud, deep honking.

Notable: Canada geese once were rare in Minnesota, but in the last ten years have been estimated at 250,000 to 350,000.

At Saint John's
Routinely gather at the Gemini Lakes and challenge anyone and anything that approaches them (including cars).

Red-winged blackbird *Agelaius phoeniceus*
• *Late Spring–Summer*

One of the most abundant birds in North America, this blackbird is often seen atop cattails, along wet roadsides, and on telephone wires. Males are glossy black with vibrant red and yellow shoulder patches that they can puff up or hide. Females are a less noticeable brown, almost like a large dark sparrow. Their loud, screeching *conk-la-ree!* song is a sign of spring.

Notable: Red-winged blackbirds fiercely defend their territories during breeding season. It is not uncommon for them to spend more than a quarter of daylight hours in defense.

At Saint John's
An ever-present companion in the wetlands. Children often question this bird's name. How is it a blackbird if it has red wings? Then they get a closer look at its bright red shoulder patch.

Oak Savanna

Prairie and oak savanna are rare today in Minnesota. Only about 1 percent of the state's original prairie survives, and only one-tenth of 1 percent of it is original oak savanna. The landscape here changes quickly season to season. Each species of flower blooms in turn over the spring and summer; grasses reach over one's head by midsummer. Prairie fires in spring and fall leave dark black pools of burnt grass, quickly replaced by green in early summer. The restored habitat attracts some forty-five species of waterfowl, songbirds, and furbearers.

Oak savannas are among Minnesota's most endangered habitats. The Abbey Arboretum's oak savanna, like our prairie, is "constructed" and restored. The area could have been an oak savanna sometime in the past five hundred years, but an 1858 survey shows the closest savanna was near Saint Joseph. The area of the Abbey Arboretum that is now an oak savanna was once a cow pasture. The monks cleared most of the trees for grass but left some scattered oaks for shade. The open spacing of these remaining oaks allowed them to develop widespread crowns typical of oak savannas. When the land ceased to be used as pasture, maple, ironwood, and basswood seeded in between all the larger trees. Father Paul Schwietz cut those "infiltrators," beginning in the 1980s, leaving the old shade oaks. He also interseeded a mix of prairie grass. After several burn-offs since then, we have the beautiful oak savanna we see today.

The care of the Earth is our most ancient and most worthy, and after all, our most pleasing responsibility. To cherish what remains of it and to foster its renewal is our only hope.

—Wendell Berry

Gunther's Garden

On the southeast shore of East Gemini, Father Gunther Rolfson, O.S.B. (1917–2004), scattered a botanist's ark of plants he gathered across the country. He began the wildflower preserve, from the shore of the lake to the top of the steep slope, as part of a project with students from Saint John's University and the College of Saint Benedict, and included seeds from both the students' study and his collection from the biology department greenhouse.

Gunther's Garden, or the Gemini Botany Reserve, initially held more than 450 species of flowering plants, though some species have disappeared with flooding or overcrowding. Father Gunther's favorite was the cardinal flower, a native perennial with bright red flowers on unbranched spikes. You can see most of these flowers in the spring and early summer; they're especially beautiful in the warm light of the setting sun across the Gemini Lakes.

North Fork of the Watab River

Three of the most visible lakes at Saint John's are actually a dammed river known as the North Fork of the Watab River. The Watab begins upstream from Stumpf Lake about a mile southwest of Pflueger Lake, circled by cattails. After exiting Pflueger, it flows for less than fifty yards in its original stream-bed and widens into Stumpf Lake, also fed by a deep aquifer and underwater springs.

Stumpf Lake Reservoir

Natural springs feed Lower Stumpf Lake near its southeast corner. When the water rose, many trees were left standing in or under water, and the reservoir was named Stumpf Lake (German for stump). Pioneer Benedictines dammed the Watab River for the first time in 1868. The water powered a flour mill, and a small sawmill for cutting large logs into the beams and boards that rib many of the older campus buildings.

A Dream of Trout

In the early twentieth century, the monks—led by Father Bruno Doerfler, O.S.B., and later, his brother, Father Hilary Doerfler, O.S.B.—used Stumpf Lake to create a small pool for a fish hatchery and a trout pond. The conditions for breeding thousands of trout fingerlings were ideal: a steady flow of water from the underground spring, a stable water tempera-

ture of fifty-five degrees, and "an almost natural terrace" where Father Hilary built a corral for the trout. Years later, during the winter, wrote Father Gunther Rolfson, O.S.B., "watercress spread out in a rich green carpet over the pond, and clouds of vapor rose from the open pools." By 1909 the hatchery had some fifty-thousand trout fry and was a major attraction. On summer evenings, the monks often fed live frogs to the trout. There is no evidence today of this fascinating enterprise: it succumbed to dry spells and vandals who couldn't resist the trout.

At a narrow point in the middle of the lake, a walking bridge (below) crosses to the Watab picnic grounds. You can look down from this causeway footbridge to spot fish that attract terns and eagles. The fill leading to this bridge contains

earth excavated during the building of the Abbey Church (1960). On the west side of Stumpf Lake on a peninsula near the lake, you can enjoy the Watab picnic grounds, site of many "Pinestock" concerts. If you follow a trail on the shoreline nearby (please see map, p. 40), you'll find gnawed trees and an old beaver lodge near the water.

East and West Gemini Lakes*

In 1966 the North Fork of the Watab River was dammed again near what is now the oak savanna, creating East Gemini Lake as a settling pond for the wastewater treatment plant required by a growing and modernizing campus. Much of the phosphorous from wastewater treatment settles to the bottom of East Gemini, causing the lake's "cyclic excess algae growth," giving the lake its green tint.

Through a drain under the county road, the raised water also fills the smaller West Gemini Lake, creating more wildlife habitat. In 1988 a third dam was built near Wimmer Pond to create wetlands as part of the habitat restoration project. You can cross this wide shallow wetland on a boardwalk that bends with the force of the flowing river (please see p. 34). Sunfish, bass, and painted and snapping turtles are common in Stumpf and Gemini lakes. Loon pairs have nested on the Abbey Arboretum's lakes for many years.

* The lakes were named when the United States was conducting the Gemini manned space flights in the mid-1960s; "Gemini" refers to the twin brothers of Greek mythology, Castor and Pollux.

Abbey Energy

The sun rises and the sun goes down, and hurries to the place where it rises.

—Ecclesiastes 1:5

The Abbey Energy solar farm, just west of the main entrance off Interstate 94, was installed in late 2009 and at the time was the largest experimental solar farm in the upper Midwest. It was also four times larger than the largest solar farm in the state and generated five times more energy. It has 1,820 modules in thirty-five rows on four acres and produces 575,000 kilowatt hours a year.* That's enough to provide 4 percent of Saint John's energy a year. During the summer the solar farm can provide up to 20 percent of Saint John's peak power needs (equal to powering about sixty-five homes). The panels have a tracking system that follows the sun, increasing production another 15 percent. Because photovoltaics generally work better in cooler air, the Saint John's solar farm produces more energy than it would if it were in New Mexico. Even snow adds reflected sunlight. The university uses the panels as a teaching tool in classes and Saint John's Outdoor University staff features the solar farm in K–12 energy classes. Native grasses and flowers planted around the site incorporate it into the environment.

* More panels were added in 2014 to produce a total of 598 kilowatt hours a year.

I was visiting Saint John's during the spring and tramped out to my favorite spot in the Arboretum.

I sat on that hill for hours—almost an entire day. Listening to the chickadees chirping, the trees groaning in the wind, and the soft rustle of a fox returning to her den. I listened and listened and listened.

I realized then that what I was given in the gift of silence was worth much more than any other response. It taught me to listen closely—with the ear of my heart, as Benedict says—for God's instructions and love. It taught me that perhaps silence is something which should be pursued, cultivated, and loved.

Listen. Most of the time I don't hear a thing. But I'm reminded that sometimes it's just as important to stop and hear what isn't being said.

—Kelly Prosen, CSB '07, SOT '11

The universe unfolds in God, who fills it completely. Hence, there is a mystical meaning to be found in a leaf, in a mountain trail, in a dewdrop, in a poor person's face. The ideal is not only to pass from the exterior to the interior to discover the action of God in the soul, but also to discover God in all things.

—Pope Francis, *Laudato Sì*, no. 233

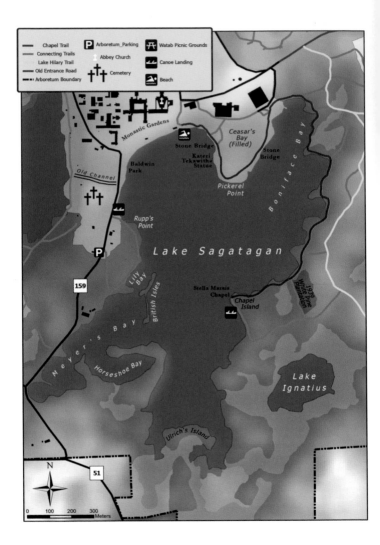

	Chapel Trail	P	Arboretum_Parking		Watab Picnic Grounds
	Connecting Trails		Abbey Church		Canoe Landing
	Lake Hilary Trail	✝✝	Cemetery		Beach
	Old Entrance Road				
	Arboretum Boundary				

Monastic Gardens

Ceasar's Bay (Filled)

Boniface Bay

Old Channel

Baldwin Park

Stone Bridge

Kateri Tekawitha Statue

Stone Bridge

✝✝✝

Pickerel Point

Rupp's Point

Lake Sagatagan

P

159

Lily Bay

British Isles

Stella Maris Chapel

Chapel Island

1939 White Pine Plantation

Meyer's Bay

Horseshoe Bay

Lake Ignatius

Ulrich's Island

N

51

0   100   200   300
Meters

Chapel Trail

3-mile round-trip • **1 hour**

Listening: To hear keenly and sensitively the voices of persons and all created beings. "Listen . . . with the ear of your heart." (RB Prol.)

The Trail

Generations of monks, students, and guests have made this perhaps Minnesota's most favored trail. Some consider it the most traversed trail in any natural setting in the state. It was first trod in the 1890s as an alternative to boating to the chapel. The trail winds near Lake Sagatagan through century-old Scots and white pine (a grove of the oldest planted trees in Minnesota), across footbridges of stone and wood, through a hardwood forest of maple, oak, birch, and tamarack. The trail is rutted and rolling, with large exposed roots and stones. Under filtered sunlight, one sees a forest bed of endless leaves, leaves freshly fallen, leaves soggy and decaying, tree seedlings emerging, trees reaching for the sky, trees decomposing into the soil. You'll hear trees swaying in the wind or rubbing

against each other. You might see a fox or spot an eagle's nest near the lake. You might hear the tremolo of an ululating loon from the lake. Or you might hear . . . nothing at all. You'll find benches for private meditation. You'll see several landmarks of Catholic devotion, including a statue of Kateri Tekakwitha, first Native American saint, a disintegrating brick staircase (once a shrine to Saint Aloysius Gonzaga), and the Stella Maris Chapel.

One of the trail's frequent visitors is Hilary Thimmesh, O.S.B. (above), who professed monastic vows in 1948, was a member of the English department from 1963 to 2008, and served two terms as university president. "Something of the quiet of thought, of solitude, of prayer without words pervades this place," he once wrote. "Not the quiet of emptiness [but] the quiet of living things, of the woods, and the lapping waters and the solitary runner . . . where water and trees and sky exert their calming influence." Runners, such as former Saint John's Prep student Kyhl Lyndgaard (SJP '95, SJU '99), also favor this trail. "I knew the placement of each rock and root by heart," he wrote, after running some seven hundred miles on the trail one summer. "When a tree fell I jumped it. I saw a coyote. I nearly stepped on a fawn that was playing dead in some tall grass. . . . I grab the same maple tree to swing from one trail to another."

The Chapel Trail begins on the north shore of Lake Sagatagan, below the Abbey Guesthouse, on the east side of the swimming beach. On this site in autumn 2015, monks and volunteers completed a timber-frame "trailhead" building, a place for gathering and reflection. The building has six fieldstone columns, capped with copper, supporting a twelve-foot high peaked roof (no nails or glue, just mortises and tenons). Timber for the structure is white pine from the Abbey Arboretum. Through tall grass and pines near the shore, the trail gradually rises to the statue of Saint Kateri Tekakwitha. A large wooden crucifix, carved by Father Cornelius Wittman, O.S.B. (1828–1921), one of Saint John's pioneer monks, once stood here, now preserved in the Abbey. The monks called this promontory Adrianople, after Father Adrian Schmitt, O.S.B., who planted many of the pines here in the 1890s. As it rounds the peninsula, the trail descends over a bridge (once called the "Bridge of Sighs," named after the enclosed bridge in Venice that connects the New Prison to the interrogation rooms of the Doge's Palace) and past a small shrine that, at this writing, lacks a statue. It once held a statue of Saint Francis and, earlier, a statue of the Blessed Virgin, called "Our Lady of the Lake" after Sir Walter Scott's 1810 narrative poem. Note the vertical line in the stone beneath the statuary alcove; it marks the line back up the hill to the north where once stood the Abbey's observatory tower, now home to the prep school.

The trail passes two granite benches, with a full south-facing view of the Sagatagan at Pickerel Point (named by the monks for a sizeable catch of the fish off this shore in the 1890s). Heading north on the east side of the peninsula, the trail passes Saint John's Preparatory School and its playing fields, and over the "Prefect's Bridge" of fieldstone (below) fashioned by the monks in the late 1910s. The trail becomes slightly rocky, rising just beneath the parking lot south of the prep school dorms, then becomes flat and graded. There's a large boulder and lily pads on the right as the trail rounds what used to

be Caesar's Bay, once preferred by students as the finest place to skate on the lake because of its sheltered landscape. In 1893 the "scholastics" dug a canal here connecting Caesar's with Boniface Bay. Caesar's Bay may have begun filling in naturally over the decades. It still appears on a 1945 map. It was filled in completely with dirt excavated from the site of the current Saint John's Preparatory School.

The trail bears right, with exposed roots, then becomes smooth as it crosses a floating footbridge past cattails and lily pads. Two side paths to the right both end in west-facing views of Boniface Bay, after Bonifice Wimmer, O.S.B. The trail dips, curves about thirty feet above the bay, then becomes smooth and sandy. On the left is a grove of wild flowers (large-leaved aster and zigzag goldenrod), a logging road, and then the trail's first view northwest toward the campus. After wetlands on the trail's left, the trail becomes cinders and descends to a footbridge (about 250 feet) over a marsh and rises to Stella Maris Chapel. The trail to the chapel was not accessible by foot until 1892, when the monks built several bridges.

When you arrive at the chapel, pause as Mackenzie Lobby, CSB '05, did on an autumn day in 2013: "We hop up on the rock wall surrounding the church and sit there to gaze upon the lake. Shards of sunlight pierce the leafy ceiling of the forest. Overhead a flock of birds heads south."

July 29, 1956

Yesterday, spent most of the afternoon in the quiet woods behind Stella Maris reading, thinking, and realizing the inadequacy of both thinking and reading. I believe what I saw was an otter. At that end of the lake also there is a great blue heron. The lake is so beautiful it makes me feel guilty. What is there in me that makes me feel I should not have so many good things? Or, rather, not only not have them, but not even see them?

—Journal of Thomas Merton

Vegetation of the Chapel Trail

Northern blue flag iris *Iris versicolor* • *Spring–Summer*

Perennial wildflower, grows up to three feet tall. Leaves are narrow and long. Flowers are showy and large (two to three inches), purple-blue with white or yellow highlights.

Notable: The term flag comes from the Middle English "flagge," meaning rush or reed, referring to this flower's preference for wet soil along shorelines, marshes, and swamps.

At Saint John's
Watch for this flower on the shores of lakes Stumpf and Sagatagan.

Yellow pond lily *Nuphar variegata* • *Summer*

Floating lily pad; leaves oval shaped with a deep notch on one side, up to fourteen inches long and ten inches wide. Emergent flowers are yellow with a red tint at the base, one to two inches wide.

Notable: Roots can be used in stews or ground into flour. Seeds can be popped like popcorn! Native Americans used the leaves to stop bleeding.

At Saint John's
There are several species of lily pads in Minnesota. Lake Sagatagan is home to yellow pond lily (*N. variegata*) as well as white water lily (*Nymphaea odorata*) and watershield (*Brasenia schreiberi*).

Pondweed *Potamogeton sp.* • *Summer*

Submerged (underwater), perennial herbs. Leaves vary from threadlike to oval shaped and attach to flexible underwater stems. Some species have floating leaves at the tip of stem. Flowers stand above the water. Common in lakes, sometimes found in moving water.

Notable: Pondweeds are excellent habitat for a variety of aquatic life such as panfish, largemouth bass, muskellunge, and northern pike. Bluegills nest near pondweeds and eat insects and other small animals on the leaves. Walleyes use pondweeds for cover.

At Saint John's
In 1997, Minnesota Biological Survey botanists surveyed the plant life of Lake Sagatagan and identified and collected nine species of *Potamogeton*.

Bladderwort *Utricularia sp.* • *Summer*

Fine-leaved, free-floating underwater plant. Leaves are threadlike and forked, emerging from all sides of a flexible stem. Interspersed between the leaves are small, round bladders that float the plant near the surface. Yellow flowers are a half-inch to an inch wide and emerge from the water on a leafless stem, two to eight inches high.

Notable: Bladderworts are carnivorous, can eat small tadpoles and mosquito larvae.

At Saint John's

Humped bladderwort (*U. gibba*), a species of "special concern," was located at Saint John's by Mike Lee and Karen Myhre, botanists for the Minnesota Department of Natural Resources, recorded in the Natural Heritage Rare Features Database of the Minnesota DNR.

Norway spruce *Picea abies*

Coniferous tree, grows thirty to sixty feet tall. Branches are orange or straw-colored and droop as they mature. The cones are long (three-and-a-half to seven inches). Spruce differs from pine and fir by its needles. Spruce needles are attached to the branch singly and are four-sided in cross section. This species is native to central and northern Europe, not to Minnesota.

Notable: A Norway spruce is the species selected as the Christmas tree at Rockefeller Center in New York City. At the end of each holiday season, the tree is sawed for lumber and donated to Habitat for Humanity.

At Saint John's

The seeds for the Norway spruce planted along Lake Sagatagan were sent by relatives of Adrian Schmitt, O.S.B., from the Black Forest of Baden, Germany (please see p. 87). They were first planted to replace trees lost in the June 1894 tornado.

Cottonwood *Populus deltoides*

Tall, deciduous, fast-growing tree, reaches 130 feet tall. Named for its summer "snow" of cotton-like seed hairs. Thick, coarse gray bark. The Latin, *deltoides*, means triangular, referring to the distinctive leaf shape. Leaves have teeth along the margins, with a flat base and pointed tip. Cottonwoods have catkins, or clumps of small unisexual flowers that hang from the branches in spring and become fruit by early summer.

Notable: Many deciduous trees have catkins, including birches, aspens, and willows. A single tree can produce up to forty-eight million seeds, dispersed by the wind.

At Saint John's
Fifty-two inches across, a cottonwood west of the sugar shack has the largest diameter of any tree in the Abbey Arboretum.

Riverbank grape *Vitis riparia* • *Midsummer–Autumn*

Vine with stem up to eighty feet long. Bark reddish brown, leaves star shaped with rounded lobes and white undersides. Like other vines, riverbank grape is aggressive and can smother other species. Common along lakeshores and riverbanks, they can survive in sandy and rocky areas. Birds eat the grapes, helping disperse seed. Fruits are edible.

Notable: The genus *Vitis* is the Latin name for grapevines. The species name *riparia* refers to "banks of rivers" or "riparian zone," where this plant is found.

At Saint John's
Look for riverbank grapes growing on the beach house by Lake Sagatagan.

> "About the time of the first frost," wrote Father Alfred
> Deutsch, O.S.B. (1914–1989), professor of English literature,
> "these [monk] scouts are on the road checking the grape
> vines which tangle in parts of the Abbey woods and are
> free to the birds and to the monks. Birds tend to get a bit
> tipsy. Monks make jelly and stay sober."

Northern watermilfoil *Myriophyllum exalbescens*
- *Midsummer–Autumn*

 Free-floating, underwater plant. Leaves
are an inch to an inch-and-a-half long,
whorled around the flexible stem. Red
spiked flowers emerge above the water
and are inch-and-a-half to four inches
long. Milfoil reproduces asexually, primarily by budding (vegetation division).
When dried, milfoil often turns whitish.
Found in lakes, ponds, and slow streams.

Notable: The Latin *Myriophyllum* means "infinite foliage,"
referring to the many fine leaves. Several species of macroinvertebrates (tiny, aquatic insects) make their homes in the
intricate leaves of milfoil.

At Saint John's
Not to be confused with Eurasian watermilfoil (*M. spicatum*), an
invasive species that can crowd out native water plants. Only the
native northern watermilfoil has been identified at Saint John's.

Broad-leaf arrowhead *Sagittaria latifolia*
- *Midsummer–Autumn*

Aquatic perennial plant, grows to three inches. Large leaves
distinctly arrowhead shaped; underwater leaves are long

and narrow, designed to withstand water currents. Male flowers are white with three petals; female flowers are inconspicuous.

Notable: Also known as "common arrowhead" or "duck potato," ducks, geese, swans, and muskrats eat the starchy, potato-like tubers on the roots of arrowhead.

At Saint John's
Seen along the shore of Lake Sagatagan and in the wetlands along the boardwalks on the Prairie-Wetlands Trail.

Large-flowered trillium *Trillium grandiflorum*
* *Spring–Early Summer*

Flower is two to three inches across with three white petals often ruffled or wavy with a pointed tip. A single flower perches atop a two- to three-inch stalk that rises above a single whorl of three leaves. Flowers turn rosy pink with age.

Notable: The largest trillium in Minnesota, the seeds are mostly spread by ants that take the fruit to their underground homes, eat the fruit flesh, and leave the seed behind. Can be several years between seed germination and first flower.

At Saint John's
Found in several locations along the Chapel Trail, although this is one of the woodland flowers at Saint John's that has become more rare as the whitetail deer population has grown.

Wildlife of the Chapel Trail

Paper wasps *Polistes*

Slender with long legs; body three-fourths of an inch to an inch long. Brown with yellow markings on body and black wings. Paper wasps are social, their colonies divided into workers, queens, and males. Worker wasps (females that aren't queens) build intricate nests from plant material and wood fiber. Nests have up to two hundred cells where the queen lays her eggs. Paper wasps attack only when the nest is disturbed. Nests hang under branches or eaves of buildings.

Notable: Only females can sting (the stinger is a modified egg-laying structure).

At Saint John's

Look for paper wasp nests when hiking the trails in the winter. They are easier to spot (and safer to explore).

Eastern chipmunk *Tamias striatus* • *Spring–Autumn*

Ten inches long, including tail. Relative of the squirrel but smaller with black-and-white stripes on the back and sides. Long tails and small ears. Internal cheek pouches enable them to carry food to store for winter. Eats tree seeds, black cherries, and mushrooms but also preys on bullfrogs, redbelly snakes, and small birds.

Notable: Chipmunks are common and considered friendly to humans but can be aggressive with other chipmunks when defending territory.

At Saint John's

Chipmunks and squirrels may be among the most photogenic critters in the Abbey Arboretum, popular in submissions to the annual Outdoor U photo contest.

Muskrat *Ondatra zibethicus*

Not really a rat, muskrats are a common herbivore in Minnesota wetlands. Fur varies from reddish to grayish brown. Often seen swimming low in the water with a long, almost hairless tail curling behind. Muskrats eat the roots, stems, leaves, and fruits of many aquatic plants.

Notable: The muskrat and its bigger cousin, the beaver (please see p. 31), are the only mammals that build homes in the water. Unlike the beaver, the muskrat does not store food in winter. It needs to eat fresh plants every day and will make channels in mud to reach food under the ice.

At Saint John's

Muskrats burrowed into the foam floats that floated the board-walk in the prairie wetlands, probably to find an easy, warm place for a den. New ones, encased in plastic, are now used to replace the older floats as they wear out.

Painted turtle *Chrysemys picta* • *Spring–Fall*

Medium-sized turtle; three-and-a-half to seven inches long. Named for the red, yellow, and black design on the underside of the shell, called the "plastron"; upper shell is dark green to black. The head, legs, and tail are yellow and black striped. Painted turtles are the most common turtle species

in Minnesota. They feed on crayfish, insects, tadpoles, cattail, and duckweed.

Notable: Painted turtles winter in lake bottoms in mud under ice; commonly called "mud turtles."

At Saint John's
Always in search of a warm spot, painted turtles sun themselves on logs in the afternoon. Look closely as you pass by marshes—you'll be surprised how many you can find.

Blanding's turtle *Emydoidea blandingii* • *Spring–Fall*

Medium to large dome-shaped turtle; five to seven inches long. Bright yellow chin and throat, dark carapace (shell) with dull yellow specks. Lives in wetlands with shallow, slow-moving water and feeds on aquatic plants, small fish, and macroinvertebrates. Like other turtles, winters in muddy bottoms of lakes, ponds, marshes, and streams.

Notable: Threatened in Minnesota due to fragmented habitat, and automobiles. Many are killed crossing roads between wetlands and nest sites. Hatchlings are especially vulnerable but can live for over seventy years.

At Saint John's
On one of her first days of work as an environmental educator for the Outdoor U, Sarah Gainey helped land manager Tom Kroll identify and rescue a Blanding's turtle crossing the road near the four-way stop at Saint John's.

Bullfrog *Lithobates catesbeianus* • *Spring–Fall*

Largest frog in North America; three-and-a-half to eight inches long. Skin varies according to temperature, light green when warm and dark green to brown when cold. Males have yellow throats, females have white. Breeds in lakes, ponds, and streams, and spends winter dormant underwater. Named for their deep "jug-o-rum" territorial call, sounds like a roaring bull.

   Notable: In Minnesota, bullfrogs are a game animal, hunted for their legs and eaten as a delicacy. When underwater, bullfrogs can close their nostrils and "breathe" through their skin.

At Saint John's
Bullfrogs are native only in the southeastern corner of Minnesota, although populations have been established by people in other parts of the state, including Lake Sagatagan. The "loud, deep, bellowing call" of the bullfrog can be heard from the beach at Lake Sagatagan during the summer.

Largemouth bass *Micropterus salmoides*

Large fish; fifteen to eighteen inches long, one to five pounds. Olive green body with black stripe down the side and spiny dorsal fin. Females are larger than males. Eats crayfish, insects, frogs, and other fish. Ideal habitat is still water with some aquatic vegetation, though largemouth bass can adapt to a variety of aquatic environments.

Notable: Its mouth extends behind the eye, compared to the small mouth bass, whose mouth ends at the middle of the eye. Adaptable and prolific, spawns in water with firm bottoms of sand, mud, or gravel; prefers beds of rooted aquatic weeds.

At Saint John's

In addition to largemouth bass, Lake Sagatagan is home to brown and yellow bullheads (distinguished by chin barbles), yellow perch (vertical stripes), northern pikes (pointed snout), blackchin shiners, black crappie, and several varieties of sunfish (bluegill, pumpkinseed, and hybrid). The lake is not stocked; its largely undeveloped shoreline is ideal wildlife habitat.

Purple martin *Progne subis* • *Spring–Summer*

Large swallow; seven to eight-and-a-half inches long. Short, forked tail and hooked beak. Males are dark purple-blue iridescent, with brown-black wings. Females, brown and gray with a white belly. Martins catch dragonflies, damsel-flies, and other insects in flight for food. Nests in birdhouses and natural cavities, such as woodpecker holes.

Notable: "Species of concern," numbers have decreased since 1980s due to European starlings, deforestation, cold weather, and pesticides. Native Americans hung empty gourds for martins before Europeans came to North America. According to ornithologist Bob Russell, SJU '67, there are no known "natural" nesting areas for purple martins. They have always used human-provided housing.

At Saint John's

Brother Gregory Eibensteiner, O.S.B. (1934–2013), fashioned a number of gourd houses on the west side of Lake Sagatagan for a colony of purple martins. All six of Minnesota's swallow species nest in the Abbey Arboretum: Purple martins, tree swallows, barn swallows, rough-winged swallows, bank swallows, and cliff swallows.

Common loon *Gavia immer* • *Spring–Fall*

Large water bird, long body over thirty inches, black-and-white plumage, red eyes. Male and female both have a black head and bill, black-and-white back, and white necklace. Excellent swimmers and divers. In flight, slower and more hunched than ducks. Characteristic maniacal wailing and ululating during breeding season.

Notable: Loons fish for food and can dive as deep as 180 feet. Most dives last about one minute, but loons have been known to stay submerged for fifteen minutes.

At Saint John's
Minnesota's state bird; the state is home to some ten thousand loons, said to be the largest population in the nation, except for Alaska (US Geological Survey). The Abbey Arboretum has been home to "Big John," a common loon surgically implanted with a transmitter (US Geological Survey no. 55480) in 2010 to track his migration from Saint John's to the Gulf of Mexico.

Bald eagle *Haliaeetus leucocephalus* • *Year-round*

Great soaring birds with wingspans seven to eight feet. Dark brown feathers. Adult birds are unmistakable, with white head and tail, and yellow bill. Immature birds vary, with

mottled brown-and-white bodies and dark bills. Male and female alike. Voice, a high-pitched, harsh cackle. Found near rivers and large lakes.

Notable: When an eagle soars across the screen on TV and in the movies, the sound that accompanies the image usually is a red-tailed hawk call, not an eagle's.

At Saint John's

A pair of eagles have been successfully nesting near the Stella Maris Chapel since about 2010.

Lake Sagatagan

Father Bruno Riess, O.S.B. (1829–1900), and his four Benedictine confreres who founded Saint John's more than a century-and-a-half ago considered this lake the jewel of their new home. He immediately sensed its spiritual and communal value. "I was bound to acquire," he said, "this sheet of water for the monastery." The lake has held Abbey guests in its spell ever since as a sacred space for spiritual reflection and renewal. The Abbey's first buildings, the old Stone House and the five-story Quadrangle, were built close to the lake's north shore. The lake also is enshrined in the alma mater of Saint John's University ("high above the Sagatagan, towering o'er oak and pine.")

Until the late nineteenth century, however, the Sagatagan was called Saint Louis Lake, after King Louis the First of Bavaria, early benefactor of the Benedictines in America. Then in 1896, a four-page saga poem, "The Vision of the Island," appeared in the student newspaper, Saint John's *Record*, about a seven-year-old

Ojibwe boy baptized in the lake and buried on the island near a chapel built of stone "Sacred to the white-robed Maiden and her gracious Child, the Infant." The poem, credited to Father Alexius Hoffmann, O.S.B., called the lake Sagatagan ("a name by which the Chippewa [Ojibwe] Indians designated the lake . . . *Sagatagan*: punk, a fungous outgrowth on trees; used for tinder"). Sagatagan it's been ever since. Everyone today rhymes the first and third syllables with "rag" but in the mid-1930s Father Alexius, first compiler of the natural history of Saint John's, insisted the Ojibwe pronounced it Sahg-ah-*tahg*-ahn.

The best sites for viewing the Sagatagan are from the grassy slope called Baldwin Park, cleared in 1961, named for Abbot Baldwin Dworschak, O.S.B. (1906–1996), on the northwest side of the lake, south of the monastic gardens, where you have a clear view of Stella Maris Chapel, and from the Abbey Guesthouse and the swimming beach and the brick laundry (*circa* 1895), now the boathouse, just below it. From there you can walk to the head of the trail for the three-mile round-trip "chapel walk" bordering the lake to Stella Maris Chapel. Stella Maris sits on Chapel Island surrounded by a slough, just north of two channels leading to Lake Ignatius. The southern end of the Sagatagan is marsh and slough, has no trails, and is in many ways a vast aquatic garden. The western side includes County Road 159, which takes you past Ulric's Island (for Father Ulric Northmann, O.S.B.), Meyer's Bay (for a family that lived here in the 1870s), Horseshoe Bend, the smaller Lily Bay, and Rupp's Point (Rupp's General Store, where students once gathered), just across the county road from the Abbey cemetery. An elderly Native American who visited Saint John's in 1922 claimed he witnessed a skirmish here, before the Benedictines arrived, between Chippewa and Dakota who were encamped respectively on a point south of Chapel Island and on the opposite shore of the lake, perhaps Horseshoe Bend.

The "Sag" is one of the Abbey Arboretum's four natural bodies of water (with Lake Ignatius, Lake Hilary, and Wimmer Pond). Around 1870 it was briefly connected to Stumpf Lake by a channel for water power. The lake covers 159 acres, three-fourths of which is less than fifteen feet deep and contain most of its aquatic plants where fish spawn. It has a mean depth of almost nine feet and its deepest spot is forty-one feet, about halfway between the swimming beach and Stella Maris Chapel. The water is clear to about thirteen-and-a-half feet; the lake bottom is muck, sand, and gravel; and it's home to northern pike, crappies, bluegills, sunfish, bass, bullheads, and perch. The lake has no visible inlet or outlet and depends on internal springs, rain, and snow. It's kept pristine and clean: it has a shoreline of forest, no development around its shores, except for Saint John's on its north, no runoff from farms; no snowmobiles or motorboats of any kind are allowed, except for emergencies. Even gas-operated ice augers are forbidden. In the summer you can rent a canoe (Minnesota law requires life jackets) to fish or tour the lake. There is a boat landing on private Abbey land on the west shore near the Abbey cemetery, which the Abbey provides for nonmotor public use. Underwater springs near the chapel feed the lake. The Sagatagan has no apparent outflow, but its water might seep underground into the Stumpf Lake springs.

The Pines of Saint John's

The towering pines gracing the northwest shore of Lake Sagatagan are a familiar part of the Saint John's landscape. They're not, however, native to this land. Not recently, at least. Most of the pines you see at Saint John's today were planted.

When the glaciers receded some ten thousand years ago, the line of conifers retreated to what now is Little Falls in central Minnesota. It wasn't until the late nineteenth century, four decades after the arrival of the Benedictines who founded Saint John's, that many of the first of these pines were planted. It started with a tornado, which tore across the Sagatagan the evening of June 27, 1894, and smashed through the campus. "The air was filled with flying timbers, furniture, limbs of trees." No lives were lost but several buildings and a forest area (where the prep school now stands) were leveled.

The monks suddenly had an opportunity to reimagine part of their forest. Father Adrian Schmitt, O.S.B. (1864–1940), descendant of foresters from the Black Forest (*Schwartzwald*) in Baden, Germany, wrote to his forester father and brothers. They sent him conifer seeds by sailing ship, and Adrian established a nursery of thousands of seedlings by Stumpf Lake. He also gathered white pine seed, probably from the Sartell or Little Falls areas. Starting in 1896, Father Adrian and his confreres planted seedlings of red pine, Scots pine, and Norway spruce across ten acres, near today's prep school and on what came to be called the Pine Knob. The conifers reminded them of their homeland in Bavaria and Austria, and their presence stabilized the Sagatagan shoreline. They grew fast; ten years later many of them were eight to ten feet tall; by 1931 they averaged forty-nine feet tall. More plantings followed in 1906, 1911, 1920, 1927, and throughout the 1930s. By one estimate in the late 1920s there were some 175,000 evergreens on the Saint John's campus. The trees that grew from seedlings planted by Adrian Schmitt, founder of Saint John's forestry tradition, today are believed to be the oldest documented reforest planting in Minnesota. Many of the pines on the northeast side of the Abbey Arboretum—now bordering I-94 and the old entrance road to Saint John's, and the area near

Stella Maris Chapel—were planted in the 1920s and 1930s by Brother Ansgar Niess, O.S.B. (1891–1981), and his confreres.

In 1926 and 1927, he and others planted 14,000 seedlings of white pine, white spruce, and Douglas fir in these areas. Brother Ansgar raised the seedlings in the Abbey nursery, then planted white pine, red pine, and Scots pine seedlings in thick rows about three feet apart, recommended at that time to encourage natural pruning and height. Interstate 94 meant the demise of many of the red pine, but you can still see some of them in the Interstate 94 median. The winter of 1947–1948 killed the needles of some of these 1896 trees. Two acres of these damaged trees were harvested in the winter of 1950 before they died or decayed, producing almost 17,000 board feet of lumber, some of which the Abbey carpenter shop transformed into 222 study tables and 111 double wardrobe cabinets for Saint Mary Hall.

In the 1970s, crews led by Brother Mark Kelly, O.S.B., thinned out some of the older pines that were diseased, rotting, or where growth was too thick to allow enough sunlight. About the same time, they planted some 20,000 seedlings in the area, including black walnut and soft maples. Some of the Abbey Arboretum's forest requires trimming to stay healthy. Late in his life, Father James Tingerthal, O.S.B. (1934–2009), using ladder and bow saw, pruned some 800 trees.

Abbey Guesthouse

Overlooking Lake Sagatagan and the head of the Chapel Trail, the Abbey Guesthouse helps fulfill the Benedictine mission to receive all guests as Christ. It is surrounded by flame grass (*Miscanthus sinensis purpurascens*), prairie dropseed grass (*Sporobolus heterolepis*), ruby daylilies (*Hemerocallis*), and flowering "red jewel" crab apple trees. Flame grass grows from three to four feet tall; has green, mounded foliage in the spring that turns reddish-purple in summer. Prairie dropseed grass forms an arching foliage fifteen to eighteen inches high; its fine-textured green leaves turn orange in autumn and light bronze in winter. Ruby daylilies are a durable perennial with grass-like leaves that produce clusters of deep, wine-red blooms on tall stems, growing fourteen to eighteen inches high. *Hemerocallis* comes from the Greek for *hemera* (day) and *kallos* (beauty). The "red jewel" crab apple tree is deciduous, its pink buds producing fragrant white flowers in midspring, and its pointy leaves turning yellow in autumn. A rain garden, downslope from the guesthouse terrace, collects rainwater from the building's footprint. This captures most of the runoff from rainfall, which soaks into the soil rather than flowing into Lake Sagatagan.

Preparatory School

The Benedictines founded Saint John's Preparatory School in 1857, building a log cabin near the Mississippi River. You can see the prep school's modern buildings today as you walk the first segment of the Chapel Trail. They're nestled into the hillside to conserve energy; all classrooms face the forest and Lake Sagatagan. The large Norway spruce and mixed pine trees between the lake and school are considered the first large-scale tree plantings both at Saint John's and in Minnesota. Slopes leading down to a wide, flat field between the school and lake are near where some of the first clay deposits were excavated by the pioneer monks for bricks for the five-story Quadrangle (completed in 1886). Horses pulled a plow-like shear through the clay, which was cut into bricks and fired in nearby wood kilns.

> Hail, Star of the sea,
> Great Mother of God
> and always a Virgin,
> joyous gate of Heaven.
>
> —*Ave Maria Stellis*,
> ancient plainsong hymn

Stella Maris Chapel

In the summer of 1872, Father Vincent Schiffrer, O.S.B. (1843–1929), and some younger members of the Abbey built a small chapel on an island on the southeast shore of Lake Sagatagan. It was Gothic in design with brick as ornament, sixteen by twelve feet, with a white wooden spire. They named it Stella Maris, Star of the Sea, in honor of the Blessed Virgin. "It was a sunset picture so exquisite," said one visitor from Austria, "from its height the little chapel looked calmly upon the scene." Light-

ning and a fire destroyed the chapel in 1903, but the monks built a new one of Romanesque style and red cement brick. It was designed twelve years later by Father Gilbert Winkelman, O.S.B. (1889–1947), who taught architecture at Saint John's, to be on the same foundation with a steeple and a balustrade of white steps leading to the shore.

In 1943, Father Cloud Meinberg, O.S.B. (1914–1982), an architect before he joined the Abbey, and a team of monks added buttresses and stained glass. The chapel was renovated in 1989; and in 2007, as part of the 150th anniversary of Saint John's, with a gift from Donald Hall, SJP '55 and SJU '59, the buttresses were removed, the inside was plastered, the outside stuccoed (led by architect Edward Anders Sövik of Northfield, Minnesota), the floor covered with Mexican tile, new stained glass (designed by Dietrich Spahn) and new doors were installed, and a bronze statue of a pregnant Mary was unveiled (designed by Alexander Tylevich of Saint Paul).

Saint Kateri Tekakwitha Statue

Along the walk to the Stella Maris Chapel you'll find a statue of Saint Kateri Tekakwitha (1656–1680), the "Lily of the Mohawks," and first Native American saint. The statue was a gift to Saint John's on the 300th anniversary of her birth in 1956 by Father Leonard Cowley, pastor of Saint Olaf Catholic Church in downtown Minneapolis. The statue had stood outside Saint Olaf before fire destroyed the church in 1953. The statue's presence in the Arboretum is fortuitous: the Catholic Church recognizes Saint Kateri, with Saint Francis, as a patron of the environment. She also is a bridge of sorts between indigenous and European cultures. She was an Algonquin Mohawk in present-day New York State. Her parents died of smallpox when she was four. Disfigured by the disease, her eyesight limited (Tekakwitha roughly translates "the one who walks groping her way"), she was baptized by the Jesuits at the age of twenty, took a vow of chastity, and lived in prayer, penitence, and service to the sick and elderly. Her statue overlooking Lake Sagatagan said "saint" decades before she was canonized on October 12, 2012.

Finding God in the Forest

Sister Remberta Westkaemper, O.S.B. (1890–1988), of Saint Benedict's Monastery in Saint Joseph, Minnesota, was a pioneer botanist, known to friends as "Remy." She was born in Spring Hill, Minnesota, received her bachelor's degree from the College of Saint Benedict in 1919 and her master's (1922) and doctorate (1929) from the University of Minnesota. She helped develop the natural sciences department at CSB, collected plants extensively in Stearns County, and preserved more than six hundred plants in the herbarium. She was the

first full-time president of the College of Saint Benedict (1957–1961) and taught biology and physiology. On field trips she was known to be able to outwalk any student, her theory being that the faster she walked the less tired she would be. She kept hard candy in her pocket to give to her students in the field when they needed energy and wore blue high-topped tennis shoes in the field, the same pair of shoes from at least 1952 until the day she retired in 1973. Saint Benedict said, "Listen with the ear of your heart," but to that Sister Remberta would have added, "Stop, and look too." Echoing Bernard of Clairvaux, she said, "You find God more in the forests than in the books. Woods and stones will tell you things you cannot hear from teachers."

> Lord, take me by the hand
> And walk with me. Amen.
>
> —Kate E. Ritger, CSB '03, SOT '07

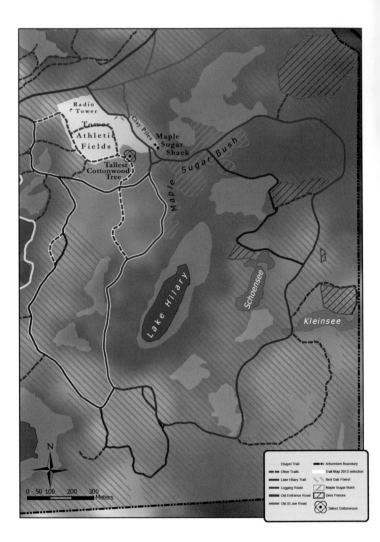

Radio Tower

Tower

Athletic Fields

Clay Piles

Maple Sugar Shack

Tallest Cottonwood Tree

Maple Sugar Bush

Lake Hilary

Schoensee

Kleinsee

N

0 50 100   200   300
Meters

Chapel Trail
Other Trails
Lake Hilary Trail
Logging Road
Old Entrance Road
Old St Joe Road

Arboretum Boundary
Trail Map 2012 selection
Red Oak Forest
Maple Sugar Bush
Deer Fences
Tallest Cottonwood

Deep Woods Trail

3.5-mile loop • **90 minutes**

Justice: To work toward a just order in our immediate environment and in the larger society. "That in all things God may be glorified" (1 Peter 4:11 in RB 57).

The Trail

Most of the hike through the "deep woods" is on the "logging road." The monks have used it for decades to harvest wood for Abbey woodworking and for limited commercial sale. It's the most developed, compacted road in the Abbey Arboretum: wide, well-defined, and rolling; with relatively flat sand and a light gravel and sometimes sandy base; easy to walk and negotiate. In the best tradition of monastic stewardship, it has kept both its aesthetic beauty and its utility. It loops through a hardwood forest, wetlands, and past three small lakes. It passes through the Abbey's grove of sugar maples, tapped every spring to make maple syrup, through groves of red oak, white oak, soft maple, elm, and ash, and includes a thirty-acre stand of aspen, regenerated from a harvest in 1937.

95

The forest of the Deep Woods Trail has a thick, leafy canopy (*schirmholt*) in the summer. You'll see a number of wind-blown, downed tree trunks left to rot on the forest floor in their natural state.

Because it's relatively smooth and rolling (save for occasional small boulders and some erosion from heavy rain) this trail often is used for high school and college cross-country races and five kilometer walks in the autumn. Father Dale Launderville, O.S.B., a theology professor, has been running this trail for more than thirty-five years and marvels at its beauty. "Cushioned paths strewn with hidden stones and tree roots keep aging bones up and running," he wrote recently. "The wall of trees in their quiet beauty as they loop through their leafed and unleafed phases lift up the spirit and protect me from icy, cold wind and burning sun. The clear, crisp air revives the body and clears the mind."

The only access to the Deep Woods Trail is from the gated asphalt road that once was the main entrance to Saint John's (off old Highway 52; pre-Interstate 94). If you've driven to Saint John's, you may park your car near the Saint John's Prep campus and enter the old entrance road eastward. Walk for about a quarter mile, past the Old Stone Gate on the right. Go right, or south, up a dirt road (above). To the left in the forest you may see a faint trace of the old Saint Joe Road which wound through the forest to Saint John's in the late nineteenth and early twentieth centuries.

Pass the 400-foot radio tower (birthplace of Minnesota Public Radio) and the tower athletic fields. At the top of the rise, ahead to the left, are the blue metal roof and aluminum smoke stacks of the sugar shack, where the Deep Woods Trail begins. Just south of the sugar shack, the trail veers right and follows the logging road east, passing sugar maples with drilled "spile" holes, and wetlands to the south. Trees with painted stripes are marked for cutting.

The road rolls gently uphill, becomes a bit rocky, straightens east, past a large boulder (remnant of receding glaciers) on the left. The elevated road descends across a wetland with a pond and cattails on the left, home to painted turtles visible in the summer. Monks created this wetland habitat in the 1960s by damming the watershed.

The road curves right (south), through a grove of red oaks, with interstate traffic visible to the east. It then passes through a marsh dominated by ash with their spare, symmetrical branches; last tree to leaf in the spring, first to shed in fall. The trail approaches a small grassy clearing then an open area of woodpiles and a nine-foot tall fence, built in 2011 to protect oak seedlings from browsing deer.

The road rises westward, past spur paths, left and right, and Kleinsee (German: "small lake") Lake (above) to the south, then angles southwest and west. This area includes the northwesternmost stand of red and white oak in the United States. The road straightens west, through large wetlands with cattails, rises and curves north and up to "John's Landing," a broad clearing where timber is loaded onto trucks. The road curves left with a view of Lake Hilary below to the east. Bird-watchers in this part of the arboretum—the so-called "Cerulean Junction"—might see or hear the light blue cerulean warbler (*Setophaga cerulea*), which nests in tall, deciduous trees and is known for its distinctive buzzing song: *zray zray zray zray zeeee*. It's a species of "special concern" across the United States but is doing quite well in our woods.

The trail goes right at the "T" and becomes a road that descends into wetland through tall canary grass, veers right, rises to the east, through a grove of oak, past more wetland, and back to the sugar shack.

> As a deer longs for flowing streams,
>   so my soul longs for you, O God.
> My soul thirsts for God,
>   for the living God.
> When shall I come and behold
>   the face of God?
>
> —Psalm 42:1-2

Vegetation of the Deep Woods Trail

Sugar maple *Acer saccharum*

Deciduous tree, up to one hundred feet tall. Bark irregular, brown to gray. Leaves three to six inches long, shaped like a star or palm, with long petioles (leaf stalks). Maples are among the few trees in Minnesota that have opposite branching (most have alternate). Other native maples at Saint John's are red maple (*Acer rubrum*), silver maple (*Acer saccharinum*), and box elder (*Acer negundo*).

    Notable: All maples are very shade tolerant and can live in the shade of their parents for decades while only growing twelve to forty-eight inches above ground, patiently waiting for a hole to develop in the canopy that will bring light needed to grow to full size.

At Saint John's

Since 1942, the monks of Saint John's Abbey have managed and tapped maple trees on the logging loop for syrup. The Native Americans used the land for the same purpose; the local name for these hills when the monks arrived was "Indianbush."

Basswood *Tilia americana*

Deciduous tree, growing singly or in a cluster with other basswood trees, up to 120 feet tall. Basswoods have alternate

branching, with furrowed ridges in the gray bark. Distinguished by large, heart-shaped leaves. Basswood fruits are round and pea sized and attached to a modified leaf that functions as a sail to aid in dispersal via wind.

Notable: Another common name for *Tilia americana* is linden. Basswood flowers in May–June and sixty-six species of pollinators have been identified on the flowers. Honey made from basswood is very light colored and considered a prize by beekeepers.

At Saint John's

The trees shading the statue of Saint Benedict in front of Humphrey Theater are littleleaf lindens, the European variety. Fr. Adrian Schmitt, O.S.B., planted a lovely lane of basswood on the knoll beyond Adrianople bridge (see p. 67) that was called "Dreizehn Linden" (thirteen lindens). Shade tolerant, basswoods have recently flourished even more at Saint John's than the Abbey Arboretum's signature red oak.

Ash trees *Fraxinus sp.*

Minnesota is home to three species of ash trees: white, black, and green. Black and green ash are ecologically important in Minnesota forests, making up more than half of the forest cover. Black ash is slower growing and prefers cool, moist places. It grows thirty-five to seventy-five feet. Green ash is faster growing and can reach forty to sixty feet tall. Bark of ash trees has deep, somewhat diamond-shaped furrows, opposite branching and compound leaves with seven to eleven leaflets (black ash) or seven to nine leaflets (green ash). White ash is found in Minnesota only in the southeast.

Notable: The emerald ash borer is a nonnative invasive insect first discovered in the United States in 2002. It threatens to kill virtually all of Minnesota's ash trees. Learn more about it from the Minnesota DNR.

At Saint John's

Ash seeds from the Abbey Arboretum and across the state have been collected and sent to University of Minnesota researchers to be saved until the emerald ash borer can be controlled.

Red maple *Acer rubrum*

This common maple has the three-pointed leaf shape of the maple on the Canadian flag. The bark on mature trees is fairly smooth and gray with narrow scaly plates.

Notable: The leaves turn brilliant reds in fall often with various shades of green veins. Sugar maple leaves turn yellow.

At Saint John's

Red maples can be tapped for maple syrup, but Saint John's taps just the sugar maple. Red maple has a lower average sugar concentration in the sap, and because it buds out earlier than the sugar maple, the red maple usually produces less sap.

Round-lobed hepatica *Hepatica americana*

Perennial herb, up to six feet high. Leaves are deep green with three distinct, round lobes. Flowers bloom early and quickly disappear; range from white to pink to blue.

Notable: Hepatica refers to the shape of the leaves, which resemble the liver. The "doctrine of signatures," dating from the eras of Roman physicians Dioscurides (circa AD 40–90) and Galen (AD 129–217), maintained that plant parts resembling specific body parts could be used to treat their ailments. Hepatica is an ancient cure for diseases of the liver.

At Saint John's

The bloom of the hepatica signals the sugaring season is coming to a close.

Indian pipe *Monotropa uniflora* • *Summer*

White perennial plant, grows to six inches tall. Often mistaken for a fungus, Indian pipe is a flowering plant. Stems culminate in a single nodding flower. During the growing season, the plant is entirely white; dried stalks are dark brown. Grows in clumps; found in mesic-hardwood habitats in low light.

Notable: Indian pipe lacks chlorophyll and therefore cannot make its own food via photosynthesis as green plants do. Instead, this unique plant is "mycotrophic," meaning it gets nutrients through a fungus intermediate (myco-fungi). Because it does not directly depend on sunlight for food, Indian pipe can grow in the dark.

At Saint John's

Keep an eye out for this unique flower. It has been spotted in recent summers in the woods behind the football field and along the Chapel Trail.

Jack-in-the-pulpit *Arisaema triphyllum*

Perennial herb, grows to about two feet tall. Has three large leaflets with a vein along the margins. Named for its unique flowering stalk ("spadix"). At its base are either male ("Jack") or female ("Jill") flowers, enveloped by a maroon-shaped leaf ("spathe"), resembling a pulpit from which a Jack or a Jill might preach. Female flowers (Jill-in-the-pulpits) develop into large bright red berries in autumn. Found in rich maple forests, sometimes in wet forests.

Notable: All parts of this plant have raphide crystals, which are needlelike and produce a numbing effect when eaten by browsers.

At Saint John's

Following a thirty-acre prescribed burn in 2003 near the logging road for oak regeneration, Jack-in-the-pulpits were especially prolific for several years.

American ginseng *Panax quinquefolius*

Woodland herb, grows to two inches tall. Three leaves emerge from a low stem and are divided into five leaflets each. Leaflets are toothed and arranged palmately (lobes radiating from a common point, like the fingers of a hand). Green flowers grow in a rounded cluster and are borne from a single stalk at the leaf axil (angle between the branch and leaf). The flowers have a slight scent of lily-of-the-valley and develop into red berries.

Notable: The genus *Panax* comes from the Greek *pan* meaning "all" and *akos* meaning "remedy." American ginseng roots are shaped like the human form. The "doctrine of signatures" considered it beneficial to all parts of the body.

At Saint John's
Ginseng once was more common in Minnesota but is now considered for listing as a threatened species due to overcollecting for medicinal purposes. Only a few plants are known to exist at Saint John's.

Zig-zag goldenrod *Solidago flexicaulis* • *Summer–Fall*

Herbaceous plant, grows to three inches tall. The common name refers to the zig-zag stem. Broad, toothed leaves come to a point at both ends. Flowers grow in clusters where the leaves attach to the stem and at the top. Common in deciduous, wooded habitats.

Notable: Look closely at the leaf stalks of zig-zag goldenrod and you'll notice tiny wing-shaped structures at the base of the leaves.

At Saint John's
This shade-loving plant is a sign of a rich forest.

Northern maidenhair fern *Adiantum pedatum*

Delicate, fan-shaped fern; grows eight to twenty inches tall. This attractive fern has dark shiny stems (rachis) and light green leaves (pinnae), arranged in a semicircle to look like the hair of a maiden. Grows in moist, shaded forest habitats and at the edge of swamps.

Notable: Ferns differ from flowering plants and conifers as they reproduce using tiny *spores* instead of seeds and cones. Many species grow well under cultivation and are used as attractive landscaping plants.

At Saint John's

Other native perennial ferns to look for in Saint John's woods include the sensitive fern, interrupted fern, ostrich fern, and the lady fern. Maidenhair fern's thin, wiry, dark stems make them nearly invisible against the backdrop of the forest floor. The leaflets look like they're floating in midair—a very graceful plant.

Giant puffball mushroom *Calvatia gigantea*

- *Summer–Autumn*

Produces perhaps the largest fruit body of any fungus. Appears in late summer and autumn, creamy white, smooth round globe often the size of a football and larger. As it matures, the flesh becomes yellowish and then dark green-brown as the spores develop. The fruitbody fills with a mass of powdery spores that, when the outer wall breaks down (or is stomped), produces a cloud of spores (hence, puffball).

Notable: Perhaps the most prolific of all fungi, and perhaps of all organisms. Total number of spores produced by a single, average-sized fruitbody is estimated at seven trillion. Spore viability, however, is very low, some experiments reporting a germination rate of less than 0.001 percent.

At Saint John's
One of the easiest fungi to confidently identify for novice mushroom hunters, it has no lookalikes. Edible when young and creamy white throughout (please see p. 127).

Grant me open ears to listen to your word in all creation.

—Christian Breczinski, SJU '98

Wildlife of the Deep Woods Trail

Mourning cloak butterfly *Nymphalis antiopa* • *Spring–Fall*

Medium-sized butterfly, a span of two to four inches. Upper side is brown to purple with a pale yellow border and iridescent blue spots along inner edge of the border. Adults mate in the spring. Caterpillars live communally and feed on young leaves, pupate, and emerge as adults in midsummer. Found with host plants, including oaks, aspen, birch, and willow.

Notable: Mourning cloaks get their name from their dark wings, resembling funeral attire. Imagine someone walking on

a dusty road in a dark cloak—the bottom of the cloak as it drags would appear to be painted tan or yellow like the wing margins of this butterfly.

At Saint John's
During the Outdoor U insects class, students learn about the phases of butterfly metamorphosis through a game in

which student volunteers dress as an egg, caterpillar, chrysalis, or butterfly and put on a brief "life of a butterfly" play for the rest of the class.

Snowy tree cricket *Oecanthus fultoni* • *Summer–Fall*

Medium-sized cricket, less than one inch. Pale green body, with pale antennae and appendages. The length of the black markings on the antennae distinguish snowy tree crickets from their close relative, Riley's tree cricket. Snowy tree crickets live on trees, shrubs, and tall weeds.

Notable: Make the familiar, high-pitched, continuous chirp. Sometimes called the "temperature cricket" because you can use the chirp to estimate the temperature: count the number of chirps in thirteen seconds, add forty to get the temperature in Fahrenheit.

At Saint John's
During a "listen-up" activity with kindergarteners, Outdoor U naturalists ask the students to be quiet and listen for at least ten seconds. Crickets are often one of the first sounds breaking the silence.

White-tailed deer *Odocoileus virginianus* • *Year-round*

Bulkier appearance in winter due to thick, warm coat. Tail and ears are used to communicate with other deer. Only bucks grow antlers, which are shed in December and grow anew during spring and summer. Most of their diet is dogwood, white cedar, and hazelnut shrubs, but they also eat mushrooms, wildflowers, acorns, and field corn. Natural predators include coyotes and bobcats.

Notable: White-tailed deer can sprint up to thirty miles an hour, leap over an eight-foot fence, and long jump thirty feet.

At Saint John's

The Abbey Arboretum hosts a regulated archery hunt each autumn to help control the deer population by focusing on removing females. The current population varies from fifteen to thirty deer per square mile. The population needed to ensure forest regeneration is eight to ten deer per square mile. To counter deer browsing of vegetation, nine-foot deer fences and plastic tree shelters protect regenerating tree seedlings.

Red fox *Vulpes vulpes*

Fifteen to sixteen inches tall and about four feet long (including the tail), the red fox is a cousin to the dog. They live in ground dens or brush piles and are especially active at night. Common throughout Minnesota, adaptable to a variety of habitats from open fields to mature forests. Diet varies widely from small rodents, birds, snakes, and fish to insects, berries, nuts, and seeds.

Notable: Red foxes bark much like dogs and can scream when alarmed. They can run thirty miles an hour and can leap fifteen feet—farther than a kangaroo.

Young foxes, or kits, are naturally curious and are popular in trail lore of the Abbey Arboretum: from the monk who had a fox lead him down the trail for several minutes as if leading him home, to the fox who was seen daily sitting on the edge of the road for weeks, as if monitoring the comings and goings of visitors to Saint John's.

Spring peeper *Pseudacris crucifer*
- *Spring–Fall*

Small frog, three-fourths to an inch-and-a-fourth long. Skin varies from tan to gray to brown; color changes with temperature. The Latin name *crucifer* means "crossbearer" and refers to the distinctive dark "X" on the spring peepers' back. Found in deciduous and coniferous forests, especially in wet places.

Notable: Given their common name for their loud, high-pitched peeping song, often heard in wetlands and seasonal ponds during spring.

At Saint John's
As the ground and water thaw during maple syrup season, the sounds of the spring peeper keep Saint John's "syrupers" company in the sugar bush.

Redbelly snake *Storeria occipitomaculata* • *Spring–Fall*

Minnesota's smallest snake, eight to ten inches long. Brown, gray, or black striped back with bright red to orange belly. Predators of the redbelly snake include birds, small mammals, and other snakes. They winter with other snake species in abandoned ant mounds, deserted wells, or rock crevices.

Notable: Redbelly snakes are not poisonous; they have tiny teeth but are harmless to humans.

At Saint John's
An especially fun snake to find when exploring with children because of the squeals of surprise and delight when they discover the bright red belly.

Sandhill crane *Grus Canadensis* • *Spring–Fall*

Large, elegant birds with long legs and necks. Thirty-six to forty-eight inches tall with six- to seven-foot wingspan. Gray to rusty brown body with black beak. Adults with red skin on crown. No distinction between male and female. Flies with neck outstretched. Migrate in V formation, similar to geese. Song a loud, rattling, bugle sound. Found in prairies and wetlands. Have bushy tail feathers and bulky bodies, which distinguish them from the great blue heron.

Notable: Were unknown in this part of the state until they started moving in from the west forty years ago.

At Saint John's
Although relatively new here, sandhills are now a favorite harbinger of spring at Saint John's, seen and heard often during maple syrup season as they nest in the wetlands near the sugar shack. You may be able to hear their primordial calls at a distance. When they're flying, these rattling bugle calls can be heard up to two and a half miles away.

Cerulean warbler *Setophaga cerulea* • *Summer*

Small, active songbird, four and three-fourths inches long. Males with sky blue (cerulean) back, white underside and white with blue streaks. Females with green-blue back, yellow-white underside and two white wing bars. Its song is buzzy notes on the same pitch followed by a higher pitched trill. Cerulean warblers nest high in the treetops of deciduous forests.

Notable: Didn't appear in Minnesota until late 1880s (from Appalachians and southern Midwest); first sighted in Stearns County in 1940s; about twenty-five pairs at Saint John's in 1965, the peak for the species before loss of habitat. Departs Panama late February, fly some three thousand miles (half of it over the Gulf of Mexico) to arrive at Saint John's in mid-May, then departs late July–early August.

At Saint John's

This species is still doing well at Saint John's and the Avon Hills. It is, however, a Minnesota species of "special concern" and the population is decreasing in its main range in the Appalachians.

Red-eyed vireo *Vireo olivaceus*
• *Summer*

Small bird, less active than a warbler; six inches long. Olive back, gray cap, black eye stripe and white eyebrow. Adult birds have dark red eyes, but this feature is not always visible. No obvious distinction between male and female. Common in deciduous woodlands.

Notable: The red-eyed vireo's song is a series of robin-like notes, first ending in an upswing (as if asking a question) then in a downslur (answering it).

At Saint John's
This is one of the few birds that sings during the middle of the day and even on hot days in the summer. If you hear a cheerful birdsong deep in the woods in the middle of the day, you can guess it's a red-eyed vireo.

Sugar Bush: Saint John's and Maple Syrup

In old age they still produce fruit; they are always green and full of sap.

— Psalm 92:14

Is there a theology of maple syrup? If you visit the Abbey Arboretum in March and April for the annual harvest of maple sap and the distilling of pure maple syrup you certainly will experience the Benedictine values of community, hospitality, and stewardship as the Saint John's Outdoor University welcomes hundreds of volunteers to join in this annual rite. The Benedictines inherited it from the Ojibwe, who tapped the maples of the "sugar bush" centuries before Europeans arrived. "Large areas were covered with sugar maple trees," wrote Father Alexius Hoffmann, O.S.B., in his 1934 manuscript, *The Natural History of Collegeville*, "which the Indians and early settlers held in some esteem. In spring they used to cut a horizontal gash into the trunk or bole and collected the sweet colorless sap, which was boiled in large pans over a fire and evaporated, leaving a deposit of soft sugar in the pans. . . . The Indians [used] to pack it into small baskets made of birch bark."

The Saint John's sugar bush is a managed grove of about 1,500 large sugar maples (*Acer saccharum*), covering twenty-nine acres near the sugar shack on the east of the Abbey Arboretum. The maples must be twelve inches in diameter to be tapped and some are as large as thirty inches and up to 130 years old.

Tapping begins in March with warm days (melting ice around pockets of gas in the trees) and below-freezing nights (contracting the gases, creating a vacuum that draws more sap from the roots). The larger the maple, and the larger its crown, the more sugar it produces. About 1,500 tapped trees produce from fifty to 500 gallons of syrup a year, depending on the weather.

The monks began harvesting maple syrup in 1942, prompted by a shortage of sugar during the Second World War, making Saint John's one of Minnesota's oldest maple syrup operations. The Abbey Arboretum team, led by Brother Walter Kieffer, O.S.B., and Saint John's Outdoor University and its hundreds of volunteers make it work today. Worker-volunteers drill holes of five-sixteenths and seven-sixteenths of an inch, slightly upward, about two inches into the sapwood and hammer a spile "or tap" into the hole. They collect sap in four-gallon plastic buckets (recycled from food service) and in plastic "sap sacks," pour it into barrels, and transport it to holding tanks near the sugar shack. The sap is boiled on a wood fire of about 700 degrees, concentrating the syrup. Maple sap straight from the tree has about two percent sugar. Every tap produces on average a quart of syrup. About forty gallons of sap make one gallon of syrup. The average maple syrup harvest lasts twenty-two days from mid-March to mid-April (the record: 560 gallons of syrup in 1985). Saint John's Abbey uses most of the syrup, giving it to volunteers and friends of Saint John's.

Average first day of collecting sap: March 19
Earliest day collected: February 26, 1999
Latest first date of collection: April 3, 1974
Earliest ending: March 24, 2012
Latest ending: April 22, 2013

"Your Gift of Sweet Sap"

Brother Walter Kieffer, O.S.B.—coleader of the syrup harvest with Dr. Steve Saupe of the biology department—has been involved in maple syrup making at Saint John's more than a half century, beginning as a freshman at Saint John's Prep in 1962. He also practices the Benedictine value of frugality as a master fix-it man and relentless recycler. For example: the slats for the sugar shack's firewood bin are boards from the university's

old hockey rink (circa 1950s). Walter wears many hats for the Abbey: monk, deacon, funeral coordinator, university faculty resident, Knights of Columbus member, woodcutter and hauler, fix-it man, and project foreman. He supervised the installation of new maple sap evaporators in 2013 and retrofitted the sugar shack with new steam and smoke stacks.

Oh, God of all goodness, of the multitude of trees you have given us in the forest, you gave us the sugar maple to provide your gift of sweet sap from the healthy trees, and fuel for the cooking from the old and culled trees. Today, following the rich traditions of our native brothers and sisters, we ask your blessing on this spring ritual. . . . May all the tap holes be clean and of a correct depth. Help us to tap the spiles correctly—hard enough to seal the spile and hold the bag, but without damaging the tree, splitting the wood and losing the sap. We ask your blessing on this season's collecting, boiling, jugging, cleanup, and wood restocking. May you reward our labors with a fruitful harvest.

—Walter Kieffer, O.S.B.
An Opening Prayer for the Maple Syrup Harvest

Tallest Tree

When you're standing at the sugar shack look west, just south of the tower athletic fields, and you can see the tallest, largest tree in the Abbey Arboretum, a cottonwood that towers over the rest of the deciduous trees in the canopy. It's 105 feet tall.

Lake Hilary

Lake Hilary is tucked far into the woods and once was a swamp with much less open water. The monks dammed the outlet of the lake, initially as a way to maintain the trail rather than to hold back water. The small dam raised the water level to about five feet at the deepest point. The dam eroded over the years, slowly lowering the lake level. Lake Hilary doesn't have fish but it does have minnows that survive the ice, which freezes to the bottom in many sections of the lake, by getting oxygen in areas warmed by spring water. The monks once called the area around Lake Hilary "Bear Swamp." Father Cloud Meinberg, O.S.B., described Lake Hilary in 1945 as being "a beautiful little lake almost one-half mile long but very narrow . . . hidden among the swaying tamaracks" with its elevated swamps on the south comprising a "great natural water garden."

Like many lowland "swamps," Lake Hilary has preserved millennia of biology in its dense, mucky bottom. In this oxygen-free environment, plant pollen, and even animal bodies and bones, may be preserved in recognizable form for countless years. By examining core samples from the lake, biology professor Dr. Gordon Brown and his students confirmed that native white, jack, and Norway pine, as well as black spruce, had existed and disappeared at Saint John's before they were reintroduced by the monks in the nineteenth century. In an area east of Lake Hilary in 2009, two white oaks were felled, believed to be the oldest in the Abbey Arboretum, one of them 242 years old, which meant it emerged as a seedling nine years before the founding of the United States of America. A slice of its trunk is preserved for classroom study in the Saint John's natural history museum in the New Science Center.

Thanksgiving in the Spirit, for a Friend

Love:
Nature-lovers sees
Through bark and water's surface:
Supernatural, grace.

—An SJU Alumnus

Controlled Deer Hunt

The forests of Saint John's are largely healthy but many areas don't have enough young trees to replace the old guard of trees and their cathedral-like canopy. Heavy browsing (eating) by large herds of deer has suppressed the growth of saplings, particularly oak, maple, and pine, and native flowers. In many areas you may see protective guards around oak trees, caps on white pine, or nine-foot high fences to help ensure at least fragments of the forest will regenerate.

In 1933 the Minnesota Department of Natural Resources, at the Abbey's request, created the Collegeville State Game Refuge on Abbey land. Hunting was not allowed and five deer were brought to the refuge to establish a local population. By 1996 the population had grown to be unsustainable, affecting the health of the deer and the forest understory. A controlled deer hunt began in 1997 to create a smaller, healthier herd and continues today as an archery hunt.

Bailey Herbarium

Father Urban Fischer, O.S.B. (1857–1927), began the Saint John's Herbarium in 1885, which later merged with the College of Saint Benedict's extensive collection of local and global plant specimens. Universities with strong biology departments have some form of stored plant collection, but this collection is distinctive for the extent to which it documents the diversity of the local ecosystem.

The CSB/SJU Bailey Herbarium is a collection of some 30,000 pressed, dried, labeled, and identified plants. It's the result of the combining of the original Saint John's herbarium, begun by Father Urban in 1885, and the Saint Benedict's herbarium, begun by Sister Remberta Westkaemper, O.S.B. The Herbarium is named after Gordon J. (SJU '57) and JoAnne Bailey, owners of Bailey Nurseries of Newport, Minnesota, one of the largest wholesale nurseries in the upper Midwest. The Bailey Herbarium is on the third floor of the Peter Engel Science Center and is open to all. It has space to study or relax in botanical surroundings, and its collections are a valuable scientific resource. Botanists from the Minnesota Department of Natural Resources and other experts have consulted the specimens for research projects, including the Stearns County Biological Survey and a study of Minnesota orchid species.

"Full of Fire and Vigor"

Father James Hansen, O.S.B. (1874–1934), was the first of many monks to use Saint John's as a laboratory for scientific investigation. He was called "a true naturalist in the best tradition of Father Gregor Mendel" (1822–1884), the Augustinian priest from Austria who founded the modern science of genetics. Father James and his students built a collection of some 30,000 insect specimens. At the time of his death, the herbarium held over 900 species of flowering plants, 300 of mosses and fifty of ferns, recognized as the region's best. "Full of fire and vigor, and gifted with an indomitable will," wrote Richard Oliver, O.S.B., Father James beat tuberculosis by spending as much time as possible outdoors studying plants and animals.

The Art of Clay

Twelve thousand years ago, when ice sheets carried clay in glacial till to present-day Saint John's, people in east Asia were experimenting with firing clay to create ceramic food storage vessels. These separate events—an epic reforming of the earth by glaciers and a modern revolution in human culture and food security—merged in 1979 when Saint John's graduate Richard Bresnahan started The Saint John's Pottery.

He apprenticed in Japan for four years with a family that had been digging local clay for ceramics since the 1500s. This tradition yielded functional artwork distinguished by the region's unique mineral mix of clay. He searched for clay in central Minnesota that had the strength and mineral profile to represent the local environment. Five miles from Saint John's, with guidance from local resident Francis Schellinger, Bresnahan found a road excavation that had exposed a high quality clay and rich ironstone usually buried too deep to access. Glaciers brought it to the surface and then left it as they receded. Bresnahan harvested this local vein and it now forms small mounds near the sugar shack. There is enough of this precious clay to provide the material for The Saint John's Pottery for three hundred years.

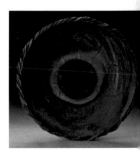

The Japanese tradition Bresnahan adapted to Minnesota avoids chemical and heavy metal glazes by using plant ash and clay to glaze pottery. Because plant species use different minerals for their cell structure, each contains a unique mineral profile. Naturally occurring silica (sand) in the plant becomes the glass, or glaze, and the trace minerals react at high temperature firing to create color embedded in the glaze. Bresnahan has used dozens of local wood and farm waste materials to create a palette of nontoxic glazes indigenous to the local ecosystem and farming community.

In 1994 The Saint John's Pottery's first kiln was replaced by the Johanna Kiln, named after Bresnahan's mentor, Sister Johanna Becker, O.S.B. (1922–2012). The largest wood-burning kiln of its kind in North America, the Johanna Kiln uses sustainably harvested, mostly deadfall trees from the Abbey Arboretum, to fire pottery to more than 2,400 degrees Fahrenheit. During the firing, ash actually melts and becomes a dynamic glaze on the pottery. This creates a finished work orchestrated by the artist and the natural vagaries of clay, kiln, and fire.

Using local and sustainably harvested clay, glaze materials, and fuel, The Saint John's Pottery brings the elements of the land into a unified voice of beauty for use in our daily lives.

A Working Woodland

Plants use the sun's energy through a process called photosynthesis. They combine carbon dioxide from the atmosphere (the C in CO_2) with water (H_2O) to create carbohydrates. This is the basis for thousands of chemical compounds in plants, including the cellulose that makes up most of the remarkable beings we call trees.

The Benedictines who founded Saint John's built their Abbey in a mature forest of northern hardwood and oak, a habitat that has grown rare in our region. As a forest ages it shades out sun-hungry seedlings such as oak and favors shade-tolerant maple and basswood seedlings. Without fire, blowdown by windstorm, or intentional harvest—cre-

ating openings with light—oak trees decrease in the landscape. Surveyor's notes from 1856 show the area near the Interstate 94 footbridge had been burned recently, probably by the Dakota, which helped to maintain oak dominance before European settlement. By rapidly harvesting timber the pioneer Benedictines actually helped perpetuate an oak forest by giving light to seedlings, which we see today in trees that are 125 to 150 years old. With their heritage and scientific curiosity, the monks followed German-based principles of forestry of their time. Their principles became the basis for modern forestry throughout the world. Monks studied and cared for the forest and led logging crews into the woods, often in full habit, to mark trees for cutting. Thanks to these pioneer monks, the Minnesota Department of Natural Resources today designates most of the Saint John's forests as excellent examples of natural ecosystems.

Look closely at the woods of Saint John's and you can see a complex forest that includes a healthy ecosystem. This includes a historic progression of different ecosystems and species. You can see trees with cavities or half-fallen "snag" trees for nesting ospreys and eagles. Buffers are left near water. Brown creepers, nuthatches, and woodpeckers eat beetles living in the snags' outer bark. Woodpeckers, raccoons, and black bears thrive on protein from the inner bark's insect pupae and larvae. Bluebirds, chickadees, nuthatches, owls, and squirrels nest in the

snags' cavities. The Abbey Arboretum tries to leave three to six snags an acre for habitat. Understory plants are protected as much as possible. Very old trees may be left untouched, despite their potential as timber, to die and decay naturally. Many so-called "quiet areas" are left unlogged and unmanaged to ensure biodiversity and to show what an untouched forest would become.

In 2002 the Abbey's woodlands were certified by the Forest Stewardship Council, verifying that the monks would continue to maintain a healthy ecosystem and harvest timber responsibly. A nearby Amish community mills the logs. The highest quality wood, about forty percent of the total harvest, is set aside for use by Abbey Woodworking, the rest is sold for flooring, pallets, and other commercial use. By maintaining sustainable use in their forest, the Benedictines reduce the amount of wood harvested unsustainably elsewhere.

The Art of Reading Wood

The pioneer monks of Saint John's were carpenters by necessity. They harvested the trees that shaped the grand buildings that still stand today and crafted their own furniture. This discipline of physical work to complement prayer and art is central to the Benedictine focus on *ora et labora*, prayer and work. The legendary craftsman among these carpenter-monks was Brother Hubert Schneider, O.S.B. (1902–1995), the master woodworker who ran the woodworking shop for more than forty years, greatly increasing its production of furniture as the campus expanded beyond the Quadrangle. "A patient teacher and an imperial critic," it was said of him, "he guided many apprentices in finding a deep respect for all the tools, organic and mechanical, put into their stewardship." The Abbey's poet-theologian, Father Killian McDonnell, O.S.B., wrote that Brother Hubert had "Braille hands" that could "read the close grain of the white oak."

Abbey woodworkers stack lumber carefully outside to let it dry. Even after years of drying, the cell structure of the wood behaves in many ways like a living being, expanding and contracting with moisture and temperature. Unlike conventional lumber, which is heated to break elements in the cell structure and minimize movement, Abbey woodworkers build furniture to allow the wood to move, giving the finished work more strength and flexibility.

The artistic vision of lay and monastic woodworkers enables them to see hidden facets of trees, the grain, and the strength of the wood. Like leaves and bark, each species of tree has distinctive grain patterns and colors. Generations of students at Saint John's University, Saint John's Preparatory School, and Saint John's School of Theology and Seminary have used desks, chairs, and beds made from oak trees grown on the land that surrounds them.

The Walnut Grove

In the 1940s, the monks planted deep in the forest a small stand of walnut trees, a prized wood for carpentry. Brother

Gregory Eibensteiner, O.S.B. (1934–2013), who was head of Abbey Woodworking from 1975–2005, was brought to this glen in his second week as a novice in the monastery in the early 1950s because he expressed interest in wood. For fifty years he occasionally walked the land to observe those walnut trees. Near the end of Brother Gregory's life, Abbey forester Tom Kroll found the walnut trees, grown to seventy feet tall, and helped Brother Gregory back to the spot for what turned out to be his final visit. Tom said Brother Gregory, in near tearful joy, touched the rough bark, thinking of the dark grains hidden behind it and what could be made in the wood shop. Still healthy and young, the trees remain for another generation of Abbey woodworkers.

The Perils of Father Godfrey

In secret caches of these deep woods Father Godfrey Diekmann, O.S.B. (1908–2002)—patristic theologian, church historian, giant of liturgical reform before and after Vatican II—foraged for mushrooms well into his 80s. As a boy, he once was found alone and paralyzed after eating bad mushrooms and had to have his stomach pumped. The experience doubtless made him a student of mushrooms; he even discovered and named a species after his brother, Father Conrad Diekmann, O.S.B. (1904–1974), a professor of English literature. Father Godfrey described excursions into the woods that brought in a daily harvest of ten or more gallons of oak or honey mushrooms. It was said he never walked into the woods without his staff and a couple of bags in his pockets or over his shoulders. "Monk walkers of all sorts seem to recognize puff ball [mushrooms] and have to check with him, stick them in his mail box, or dump them on the floor of his room," wrote

Father Alfred Deutsch, O.S.B. "More and more monks are familiar with the locally famous 'hen of the woods' [mushroom] and give him the details of their location, even drive him to the place." Wrote broadcaster, journalist, and author Krista Tippett of Father Godfrey's fungophilia: his "mushrooms . . . were the perfect metaphor for his theology: a common slogging through beauty, getting rained on, getting dirty, taking in the fields' and forests' silent declaration of God, anticipating the delicious meal

to come." For Father Godfrey (above), it wasn't really about the mushrooms. It was about the communal sharing of them in a meal. There is a story, perhaps apocryphal, that when his brother was dying, Father Godfrey asked him where his secret mushroom spot was in the Saint John's forest. Father Conrad, so the story goes, wouldn't tell him.

Father Godfrey also rejoiced in finding wild leeks, chokecherries, wild grapes, plums, high bush cranberries, puff ball mushrooms (above, and please see p. 105), and picking a bushel or more of watercress at a time, producing a most-delicious cream of watercress soup. On one of these expeditions, in September 1984 at the age of seventy-six, he walked alone as usual to the only place in the area where he knew watercress grew: on the surface of the "long-abandoned" trout hatchery in the Stumpf Lake reservoir—there could be found watercress he himself planted ten years earlier. Father Alfred Deutsch, O.S.B. (1914–1989), described what happened: "In his hip boots, from the fire department, he plunged into the mud with his brown garbage bag and his staff . . . [failing] to notice that with every bending the hip boots were minutely sinking into the eager mud. When the sack was sufficiently heavy, he flung it toward the pool edge. . . . Then he discovered he was immobilized. . . . Inch by inch the mud was swallowing him, the water was seeping over the top of his boots . . . the more he tried to unstick himself, the deeper the mud pulled him down." It was all remindful of Psalm 69:2, "I sink in deep mire, where there is no foothold." Godfrey bellowed in panic for help and Alfred, who happened to be walking in the area, heard his cry. A team of rescuers was summoned. They placed two sections of plywood over the mud and lifted the waist-deep Godfrey from what could have been his grave of mud. "What now bothers me," he wrote that Christmas, "is that during the entire ordeal of about twenty-five minutes I didn't have a single pious thought! What does that say of my more than fifty years of monastic life? Do I have to start all over again?"

> How very good and pleasant it is
>> when kindred live together in unity!
> It is like the precious oil on the head,
>> running down upon the beard,
> on the beard of Aaron,
>> running down over the collar of his robes.
> It is like the dew of Hermon,
>> which falls on the mountains of Zion.
> For there the Lord ordained his blessing,
>> life forevermore.
>
> —Psalm 133

Together with our obligation to use the earth's goods responsibly, we are called to recognize that other living beings have a value of their own in God's eyes: "by their mere existence they bless him and give him glory" [*Catechism of the Catholic Church* 2416], and indeed, "the Lord rejoices in all his works" (*Ps* 104:31). By virtue of our unique dignity and our gift of intelligence, we are called to respect creation and its inherent laws, for "the Lord by wisdom founded the earth" (*Prov* 3:19).

—Pope Francis, *Laudato Sì*, no. 69

"Praise be to you, my Lord, through our Sister, Mother Earth, who sustains and governs us, and who produces various fruit with colored flowers and herbs."

—*Canticle of the Creatures* quoted in *Laudato Sì*, no. 1

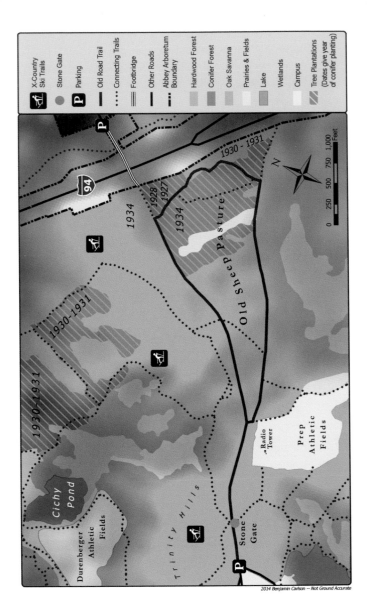

Legend

- X-Country Ski Trails
- Stone Gate
- P Parking
- Old Road Trail
- Connecting Trails
- Footbridge
- Other Roads
- Abbey Arboretum Boundary
- Hardwood Forest
- Conifer Forest
- Oak Savanna
- Prairies & Fields
- Lake
- Wetlands
- Campus
- Tree Plantations
  (Dates give year of conifer planting)

1930 - 1931

1934

1928
1927

1934

Old Sheep Pasture

1930-1931

1930-1931

Cichy Pond

Durenberger Athletic Fields

Trinity Hills

Radio Tower

Prep Athletic Fields

Stone Gate

P

N

0   250   500   750   1,000
Feet

2014 Benjamin Carlson -- Not Ground Accurate

Old Road Trail

2-mile loop • **1 hour**

Stability: To cultivate rootedness and a shared sense of mission. "To stand firm in one's promises" (RB 58).

The Trail

The Old Road Trail is a palimpsest that traces a century and a half of transport into Saint John's, from horse-drawn wagons to the hum of the interstate. If you know where to look, and look closely, you can discern the faint outline of the monks' first wagon trail (1865), which wound along gully and wetland and through the forest. You also can walk the forest path of the remains of the old Saint Joe Road (late 1880s) and the asphalt road of the "old" primary entrance to Saint John's (1927; widened and resurfaced in 1952).

In 1977, the road to Saint John's became part of the interstate highway system and a walking bridge, paid for by the government, was built over I-94 to connect with Saint John's Abbey property that the interstate had severed. You can find 400 acres of Saint John's forest and old Collegeville across this bridge, as well as the Lake Wobegon Trail, named after Garrison Keillor's *A Prairie Home Companion* radio program. ("On the Lake Wobegon Trail/Through farm and valley and dale/In the autumn sunshine/Oh, what is so fine/As a ride with your pal on the Great Northern Line?") The program started on Minnesota Public Radio, which began at Saint John's in 1967. The sixty-two mile trail, from Saint Joseph northwest to Osakis, was once owned by the Burlington Northern Railroad Company, successor of James J. Hill's Great Northern; Collegeville Station was once the arrival point for Saint John's students.

Begin by heading east from the gates of the old paved entrance road, the same starting point for the Deep Woods Trail and the Pine Knob Trail. You'll pass the

Old Stone Gate on your right, and the road on your right at the radio tower that leads up to the sugar shack. Stay on the old entrance road eastward and you'll come to a lovely stand of big tooth aspen on the right, and then pass a gated road on the right that connects south to the old Saint Joe Road. Go straight (east) on the asphalt road. You'll pass another gated connector trail on the left that turns into the Pine Knob Trail.

Continue on the asphalt road, passing wetlands to your right and then a thick stand of white pine, seeded by the older, taller pines to the south. Every "whorl" of branches on a white pine is a year of growth, so by counting the whorls you can determine a white pine's age. Vast stands of eastern white pine once covered some 3.5 million acres in Minnesota as recently as the latter half of the nineteenth century; today only about 2 to 10 percent of that original coverage remains. At the end of the asphalt road, just before a sidewalk rises to the covered bridge over the interstate, take a right (south) and follow the soft, needle-covered path as it rises gently into the elevated area of tall pines planted in 1926 and 1927.

You'll come to a juncture at which the trail splits into two paths, both of which curve gracefully through tall pines (photo, p. 131), the most mature of which are harvested by Abbey Woodworking for coffins for the monks. You'll come to a small clearing where either trail meets the leaf-covered path of the old Saint Joe Road. Here you may encounter the spirit of Brother Thaddeus Hoermann, O.S.B. (1817–1897), the Abbey teamster who drove his wagon three miles daily into Saint Joseph in the

1870s for provisions and delivered building-materials from Saint Cloud. Brother "Taddy" was a man of few words and could barely read or write, but he was a trusted, loyal provisioner, though not one to be hurried. One confrere recalled him sitting "meditatively on the seat of the springless lumber wagon with his shabby coat, broad-brimmed hat, smoking his short pipe and letting the nags amble on, convinced that his destination would wait." I could have, the confrere confessed, done Brother Taddy's journey

on foot in less time. Turn right (west) onto the old Saint Joe Road.

In the late 1920s the monks cleared the entire triangle of much of this area for a sheep pasture. In the ditch to your left you can still spot remnants of woven wire (below) marking the southern border of this pasture. The sheep venture ended after only a few years. The land likely reverted to grass and, absent any woody plants, became an ideal site for pine trees, many of which survive today. You'll come to a small clearing on the right, and if you look closely just to the east, you can spot the faint trace of the original wagon path into Saint John's, dating back to the mid-1860s.

The old Saint Joe Road was built mostly straight through the forest; workers using horse-drawn wagons had to cut-and-fill earth at several points, such as the ponds the road crosses over about halfway on your return to the starting point. You'll

pass broad wetlands on the left, a spur road on the right that connects back to the old entrance road, and an open oak forest on the left. You'll come to a juncture with a road (south) that veers left to the sugar shack. Stay right (west) on the leaf-covered old Saint Joe Road. This takes you back to the asphalt of the old entrance road.

Vegetation of the Old Road Trail

Northern red oak *Quercus rubra*

Large upland tree, grows to eighty feet tall and can live up to two hundred years in this area. Bark has deep furrows and ridges, grayish brown. Leaves have pointed lobes, each lobe coming to a bristly tip. *Rubra* is Latin for red, referring to leaf color in fall or the reddish color of the wood.

Notable: Acorns are an extremely important source of protein for forest wildlife, from insects to deer. Only one in five hundred acorns becomes an oak seedling. Most of those seedlings die before a tree is established.

At Saint John's

Seven hundred acres of our forest is predominantly red oak, much of which originated between 1870 and 1900, as the forest was harvested to build and heat Saint John's. Red oak is the most common wood used for chairs, tables, and desks made at Abbey Woodworking and used around campus.

Quaking aspen *Populus tremuloides*

Large deciduous tree, grows to 105 feet. Bark and branches whitish gray-green; often mistaken for paper birch from a distance but has smooth bark compared to the familiar papery texture of birch.

Leaves are round and broad at the base and come to a short tip, with blunt teeth along the margins.

Notable: Quaking aspen is a clonal species, meaning that several trees covering a huge area may have identical genes and an intertwined root system. This species is considered the world's second-largest individual organism, after a species of fungus.

At Saint John's

The Latin, *tremuloides*, translates to trembling, or quaking, and refers to the leaves. The leaf stalks, or petioles, of quaking aspen leaves are flattened so the leaves tremble in the wind.

Paper birch *Betula papyrifera*

Deciduous tree, up to seventy feet tall. Creamy white, papery bark. Leaves with toothed margins, egg shaped and tapering to a point at the tip. Common throughout the state because paper birch can tolerate a variety of soils. Most don't live past eighty years. Paper birch seedlings need full sun to grow, so a disturbance (fire, windstorm, or clear-cut) is required for a second generation to establish. In forest succession, maples, basswood, and spruce replace birch when they die.

Notable: Native Americans used the bark for canoes and baskets because the bark's oil makes it nearly waterproof. Wrote Alexius Hoffmann, O.S.B., in 1934: "The [paper birch's] inner bark is cinnamon-colored and grows vertically; the outer, buff in color, with a white petal, which is removed, may be taken off in horizontal rings, cut into shape, and was used for making canoes by the Indians. The sheets of birch bark, perhaps 2 x 4 feet, were sewed together with watab, a 'thread' made of thin pine roots, and the seams covered with pitch to make the canoe water-tight."

At Saint John's

There are several acres of young paper birch near the Abbey Arboretum's east property line. The area was logged in the 1980s. Birch trees on the neighbor's property provided enough seed to fill in the area to predominantly birch.

Large-leaved aster *Eurybia macrophylla*

Herbaceous plant, grows to four inches tall, with large leaves (four to eight inches wide). Often covers the forest floor. Leaves are heart shaped, hairy to rough. Upper leaves are similar in shape but smaller. Like other members of the aster family, large-leaved asters have composite flowers (ox-eye daisy is an example), with *disk* flowers in the center and *ray* flowers along the edges (often mistaken for petals). Large-leaved aster has yellow to red disk flowers with pale purple to white ray flowers.

Notable: *Eurybia macrophylla* is also known as "lumberjack toilet paper." The large, soft leaves grow in abundance in a variety of wooded habitats.

At Saint John's

A ubiquitous species, found in nearly every wooded area at Saint John's.

White snakeroot *Ageratina altissima var. altissima*

- *Summer–Fall*

Woodland herb, up to five inches tall. Broad, toothed, heart-shaped leaves on three-fourths inch petioles (leaf stalks) to

the stem in opposite branching. White flowers grow at the top of the plant in a flattened cluster in late summer. Common in wooded areas.

Notable: Nancy Hanks Lincoln, mother of Abraham, was a victim of so-called "milk sickness." She died in Dubois County, Indiana, at the age of thirty-four in October 1818, a week after drinking milk from a cow that ate this poisonous plant and passed the poison through the milk. Her son was nine years old.

At Saint John's
One of the few blooming plants in the forest in late summer.

Hog peanut *Amphicarpaea bracteata* • *Summer*

Perennial twining herb, growing to three-and-a-quarter inches tall. Leaves have three egg-shaped leaflets with smooth margins. Flowers are small, white or purple, and develop into flat peapod. "Hog peanut" is named for its underground edible pods, which develop from "cleistogamous" (underground) flowers. A member of the pea family, found in woodland areas.

Notable: "Leaves of three, let it be" is a common way of remembering characteristics of the infamous poison ivy (*Toxicodendron radicans*) but it also describes a variety of "safe" plants. Hog peanut has smooth leaflet margins on its three leaflets, while the leaflets of poison ivy often (but not always) have a few teeth, with the middle leaflet on a longer pedicel (stalk) than the other two.

Found along trails and the edge of woods. The tiny hog pea-
nuts are edible but it takes a lot of digging to find enough
for a meal.

Wild Columbine *Aquilegia Canadensis* • *Spring–Summer*

Five upside-down tubes fused at the
tips into a bell-shaped, nodding flower.
Red with yellow tips but can range from
pink to orange. Leaves are compound
in groups of three and alternate up the
stem. A shade-tolerant flower found in
woodlands.

Notable: The only native columbine
found in Minnesota. The genus *Aquilegia*
is taken from the Latin for eagle, whose
claws are said to resemble the petals of the flower.

A fun flower for naturalists to help people explore, especially
because of its sweet nectar. Caution: knowing where to find
the nectar in the flower is helpful; pollen, as it turns out, is
not nearly as sweet.

European buckthorn *Rhamnus cathartica*

An invasive, tall, understory shrub
or tree up to twenty feet high. Brown
bark with elongated silvery horizontal
lines, similar to native plum or cherry
tree bark. Leaves are dark green, glossy,
and small toothed. Leaves stay green
late into the fall. Female plants have
clusters of small black fruit resembling
dark chokecherries.

Notable: Aggressively invades forests and savannas, completely eliminating native plant diversity in the understory. Seedlings are extremely shade tolerant. Plants leaf out early in spring and retain leaves late in fall, creating dense shade. Seeds have laxative effect on birds (see Latin name *cathartica*) who disperse them. The seeds remain viable in the soil for several years.

At Saint John's

Removing buckthorn is a constant battle. It has been kept fairly contained in the Watab picnic area, but new plants are regularly found throughout the woods. In 2009, a summer crew of Saint John's students pulled an estimated 60,000 plants.

American elm *Ulmus americana*

Large trees, fifty to seventy feet tall and twenty-four to forty-eight inches in diameter. Branches are wide spreading and droop at the ends, giving the crown a vase shape. Leaves alternate on stem and are oval with a sharp point, double-toothed edges, and pronounced veins. The base of the leaf is not symmetrical. Turns yellow in autumn; winter buds are covered by brown, silky hairs.

Notable: Shade-tolerant and fast-growing trees were popular for urban forestry until Dutch elm disease, native to Europe, swept through Minnesota in the 1960s and 1970s, killing millions of elms. They still grow from seed but are susceptible to the insect that transmits the disease when the elms are about twenty to thirty years old.

At Saint John's

A very large elm that died in 2010 was in a small grove along the Lake Hilary Trail that also had very large specimens of white oak, red oak, sugar maple, and basswood. The trees in this grove were much older than their current neighbors, meaning it is possible that they existed but were all much younger (and smaller) than other trees in the 1870s when the monks were logging in the area.

Wild ginger *Asarum canadense* • *Early Spring*

A single purplish-red to brown tubular-shaped flower that grows inconspicuously close to the ground. The inside of the tube is creamy white. Each plant has a pair of basal leaves on stems up to six inches long. Leaves are heart shaped with a deep cleft at the base and are six to eight inches long and wide when the plant is mature. Plants spread mostly by underground rhizomes.

Notable: Tends to grow in colonies, the flower color makes it easy to miss among the leaf litter in the woods in early spring. Not related to the ginger plant that produces the ginger root popular in Asian cooking.

At Saint John's

In Outdoor U classes, children learn about plant adaptation and why a plant might develop a certain growing habit. A tubular flower that lies on the ground draws insects like gnats, flies, and ants to the cup-like flower to aid with pollination and seed dispersal.

> For there is hope for a tree,
> if it is cut down, that it will sprout again,
> and that its roots will not cease.
>
> —Job 14:7

Wildlife of the Old Road Trail

Stick bug *Phasmatodea*

Long, stick-shaped insect, two to four inches long. Stick bugs are plant eaters, usually found on trees, shrubs, and forests. They get their name from their slender, stick-like appearance that gives them camouflage. Females lay their eggs on a plant, and larvae hatch with food readily available. Even the eggs are camouflaged: they look like seeds. Birds and parasitic wasps are the natural predators of these insects.

Notable: The longest insect in the world is *Phobaeticus chani*, a species of stick bug twenty-two inches long (not found in Minnesota).

At Saint John's

They can be difficult to spot in a forest full of sticks but easy to spot when they were found loitering on the doors of the Peter Engel Science Building—a great opportunity for Outdoor U staff and students one summer. Since they don't have wings and walk extremely slowly, it's a mystery how the stick bugs came to be there.

Deer fly *Tabanidae*

Close cousins of the larger horsefly, deer flies are about a half-inch long. They are the persistently pesky bugs that buzz around our heads (and even get caught in our hair) on hot summer days. After eating, females lay eggs on plants sticking up out of wetlands. The larvae hatch and fall into the water where they live as predaceous worms and overwinter. Pupae develop along the water's edge in early summer and the adult stage lasts through much of June and July. Only one generation develops each year.

Notable: The name deer fly refers to its habit of feeding on white-tailed deer. Taking a closer look, the deer fly is actually quite beautiful, with transparent, patterned wings and metallic green-gold eyes.

At Saint John's
A student naturalist returned from Thailand with this helpful advice: if you carry a stick near your head, the movement keeps the flies away.

Tree squirrels *Sciurus* • *Year-round*

The Abbey Arboretum is home to three species of tree squirrels: Gray squirrel (*Sciurus carolinensis*), fox squirrel (*Sciurus nigra*), and red squirrel (*Tamiasciurus hudsonicus*). All three have bushy tails, are territorial, and store food in caches. The fox squirrel is the largest, the red the smallest. Fox squirrels have a dull orange underside and orange-gray back. Gray squirrels are the Arboretum's most common, with a gray coat and white belly. Red squirrels, pictured here, are significantly smaller and more obnoxious to humans (and to gray squirrels), and have orange-red coats with white undersides.

Notable: In some parts of Minnesota, you may see black squirrels or albino white squirrels. These are two genetic variations of the gray squirrel. You can trick a squirrel into showing itself by clicking two quarters together, which makes a squirrel-like sound.

At Saint John's

Red squirrels are territorial because they are protecting the food they store in a single location and can be found "yelling" at students on campus as they walk to and from class.

Black bear *Ursus americanus*

The black bear is the only species of bear in Minnesota and it is generally restricted to forested areas in the northern half of the state. A large black, sometimes brown, mammal with a large head, small eyes, erect ears, stout legs, and short tail. Approximately five to six feet long, adults are 150 to 500 pounds. Bears make huffing, snorting, and jaw-popping sounds when nervous or distressed.

Notable: True hibernators, bears stay in their dens for as long as six to seven months in winter, living off of stored body fat. They do not eat, drink, urinate, or defecate during this time, but females can give birth and nourish their cubs while hibernating.

At Saint John's

In 2012, a young black bear, not commonly seen, was spotted several times in the Abbey Arboretum and around campus. It even posed nicely for a trail camera set up to observe the live traps used to capture an overpopulation of opossums in the woods that year.

Common garter snake *Thamnophis sirtalis*
- *Early Spring–Autumn*

Medium-sized (typically sixteen to twenty-six inches long). Dark brown or black with three light-colored stripes from head to tail. Belly is pale green, yellow, or gray. Found in grasslands, especially near water. Widely distributed in Minnesota and the United States.

Notable: Round-eyed snakes like the garter snake generally are nonvenomous. Venomous snakes have vertical slits for eyes; however, there are exceptions. The garter snake retreats to its exact same hibernaculum (shelter such as a rock pile where it lies dormant) every winter.

At Saint John's
In addition to the common garter snake, you might also see plains garter snakes (*Thamnophis radis*) and redbelly snakes (*Storeria occipitomaculata*).

Blue-spotted salamander
Ambystoma laterale

Stout, short salamander, three to five inches long. Black back, light belly, and small blue spots on sides and back. Adult blue-spotted salamanders eat beetles, snails, earthworms, and spiders. The blue-spotted salamander is the most common in Minnesota. Found in moist hardwood forests; breed in small ponds.

Notable: To deter predators, blue-spotted salamanders release a foul-tasting substance from the base of their tails.

At Saint John's

An Outdoor U naturalist once asked a group of second-grade boys to search under logs for blue-spotted salamanders. Don't expect to find one, said the naturalist, they're *very* rare. Whereupon, one of the boys haphazardly kicked a log over to behold . . . a blue-spotted salamander.

Turkey vulture *Cathartes aura* • *Spring–Fall*

Large, soaring birds, slightly smaller than eagles (body twenty-six to twenty-seven inches, with six-foot wingspan). Dark feathers with a naked, pinkish head. Sexes alike. In flight, notice the two-toned wing feathers. The teetering V shape helps distinguish vultures from bald eagles when soaring. Often perch on dead trees, posts, or on ground, feeding on carrion.

Notable: Vultures make warning calls when they're close to their nests; otherwise they are silent.

At Saint John's

A pod of more than fifty juvenile vultures makes its home at Saint John's each summer. These birds roost together. They gather about 5:00 p.m. in large numbers on the water tower before heading to their roost.

Ovenbird *Seiurus aurocapilla* • *Summer*

Large for a warbler but smaller than a sparrow, six inches long. Olive-green back and spotted-white belly, with black-and-orange striped crown and a white eye ring. Male and female look alike. The male ovenbird sings a quick, resounding, "TEACHer, TEACHer, TEACHer." Found in deciduous and coniferous forests, from oak to maple to pine.

Notable: Ovenbirds build nests on the ground that often have a partial dome, giving them the look of an oven with an open door. Nocturnal migrants, ovenbirds fly low and are one of the most frequently found kills at communication towers and tall buildings.

At Saint John's
Territorial ovenbirds sing well into July, easily heard in the hills south of the sugar shack and west of Stumpf Lake.

Red-shouldered hawk *Buteo lineatus* • *Spring–Fall*

Medium-sized bird with broad wings and a fan-shaped tail, fifteen to sixteen inches long. These hawks get their name from the reddish-brown feathers on their shoulders. Adults have dark-and-white bands on wings and tail, with red and white undersides. Immature red-shouldered hawks have brown backs with white and brown streaked undersides. Found in larger blocks of woodlands. The most common call is a "kee-yer," the second note lower than the first.

Notable: Once considered the most common hawk in the northeastern United States, it fell victim to DDT; now rarely seen in the Midwest, a species of "special concern" in Minnesota.

At Saint John's

There are normally two pairs of nesting red-shouldered hawks in the Abbey Arboretum. Several neighbors also have nests, making this one of the more active areas in the region for red-shouldered hawks.

Black-capped chickadee *Poecile atricapillus* • *Year-round*

Small birds with a rounded head, long tail, and short beak; about five inches long. As the name suggests, they have a solid black cap and a matching bib that distinguishes black-capped chickadees from other species. Their back, wings, and tail are gray, with a buff underside and white cheeks. Chickadees live in mixed and deciduous forests, willow thickets, and residential areas.

Notable: Despite their small brains, chickadees have amazing memories. They hide food in caches for winter and can recall thousands of locations. The chickadees' song is a buzzy whistle, "chick-a-dee-dee-dee." As social birds, they are often seen with woodpeckers, nuthatches, and other woodland species.

At Saint John's

They're small but hardy. It's one species that stays in Minnesota throughout our long winters and seems to be cheerful doing so.

Apples, Plums, Grapes!

Father John Katzner, O.S.B. (1850–1930), came to Saint John's in the early 1870s and taught string, wind, and percussion instruments at the college for three decades. When a physician ordered him to spend more time outdoors, he turned full-time to horticulture. He raised seedlings in his monastery room with a southern exposure, grafted the first fruit trees in Stearns County, and experimented with some two hundred varieties of apples, sixty varieties of plums, forty varieties of pears, thirty-five varieties of grapes, and ten varieties of cherries. He also superintended Saint John's grounds from 1908 to 1924. He collected and catalogued seeds from all over the world, introduced hearty upstate New York apples to Minnesota, and created a hybrid called the "Alpha grape,"  combining a Saint John's wild grape with a Concord variety. A stand of those original grapes still grows on the pergola in the monastic gardens. "The alpha is ripe and ready for the table the first week in September," he wrote, "but if left on the vine till the end of this month it will become perfectly sweet with just a little vinous taste. This is something of real value, the more so as the vine, when well established, will stand a cold of forty degrees below zero without any protection." Ever the optimist, contesting winter to the end, he was experimenting with raising peaches when he died in 1930. North of the Abbey cemetery during his lifetime there was a prolific garden from which rose a cornucopia of carrots, onions, beans, zucchini, tomatoes, sweet corn, plums, muskmelons, watermelons, and raspberries for the monastic refectory. In the late 1980s, the monks harvested enough fruit from this garden and from wild species to produce 460 quarts of jelly.

Then God said, "Let the earth put forth vegetation: plants yielding seed, and fruit trees of every kind on earth that bear fruit with the seed in it." And it was so.

—Genesis 1:11

Saint John's First Game Manager

On July 22, 1933, Abbot Alcuin Deutsch, O.S.B., signed a contract with the State of Minnesota formally setting aside the Abbey's 2,438 acres as a state game refuge. The use of firearms on the Abbey's land thus was prohibited and game birds could be taken only through trapping or snaring. Every state game refuge requires a warden. Abbot Alcuin wisely chose Father Angelo Zankl, O.S.B. (1901–2007), for this duty, making him the Abbey's first and only game manager. Father Angelo had hunted pheasant and prairie dogs in North Dakota and was an avid angler. Wearing a game warden's sash and uniform, he patrolled the Abbey lands during the day, never arresting a game poacher but shaking his finger at a few of them. He introduced Chinese ringneck pheasants to the Abbey lands (they failed to survive, perhaps because of the winters). He also has the dubious honor of introducing deer to the Abbey's land in 1935. As a novice, he pushed the wheelchair of Father Cornelius Wittmann, O.S.B. (1828–1921), one of Saint John's founding monks. Father Angelo died in 2007, at the age of 106, after eighty-six years as a professed Benedictine monk, the longest such tenure on record.

The Monk Who "Found" Saint John's

Saint John's stewards the land it occupies today because of the foresight and persistence of Father Bruno Riess, O.S.B.

(1829–1900). He was the Benedictine missionary, Bavarian-born, who, at the age of thirty-six, filed claims for the land in the mid-1860s. "I went ahead with my compass and sighted some distant tree that stood in the direction pointed out by the compass," he wrote of his initial survey of the land. "Then I made for that tree, reckless of shrubs, thorns, and marshes. I could not mind my feet for fear of losing sight of the tree. In this way I sacrificed several pairs of trousers. I made to mark off quarter sections. With my short legs I could make only

one thousand steps to each quarter-mile. To avoid danger of losing track of my count I picked up ten chips and threw away one of them after every one hundred steps. When the chips were exhausted, I had arrived at the end of the quarter section. The brother, who followed me with an ax, marked the trees along the line. . . . I put up about twenty signs in different parts of the land I intended to claim, with the inscription: 'Application for this land is made to Congress for St. John's College.' These signs effectively kept off intruders . . . [and] we were no longer disturbed by land-sharks." Father Bruno remained in missionary work the rest of his life, died in 1900, and is buried at Saint Joseph's cemetery, Peru, Illinois.

The Saint John's campus was holy before the first monks arrived.

—Timothy Kelly, O.S.B. (1934–2010)
    Ninth Abbot of Saint John's Abbey

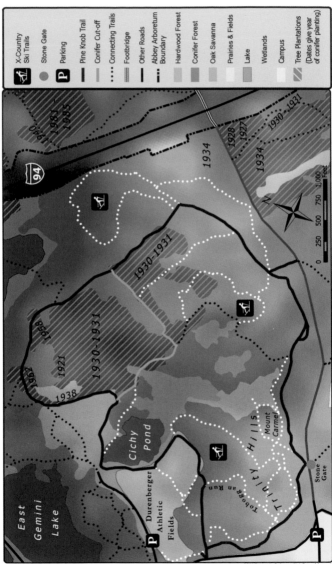

Legend:

- X-Country Ski Trails
- Stone Gate
- Parking
- Pine Knob Trail
- Conifer Cut-off
- Connecting Trails
- Footbridge
- Other Roads
- Abbey Arboretum Boundary
- Hardwood Forest
- Conifer Forest
- Oak Savanna
- Prairies & Fields
- Lake
- Wetlands
- Campus
- Tree Plantations (Dates give year of conifer planting.)

East Gemini Lake

Cichy Pond

Durenberger Athletic Fields

Trinity Hills

Mount Carmel

Toboggan Run

Stone Gate

1931
1933
1940
1928
1927
1930-1931
1934
1934
1930-1931
1930-1931
1962
1921
1938
1958

94

0 250 500 750 1,000 Feet

2014 Benjamin Carlson -- Not Ground Accurate

The Pine Knob Trail

2.5-mile loop • **60–90 minutes**

Stewardship: To appreciate and to care lovingly for all the goods of this place. "Regard all utensils as if they were the sacred vessels of the altar" (RB 31).

The Trail

The so-called Pine Knob Trail, once called pine knoll, passes through hardly any pine at all. The knob, or hill, with its stand of majestic pine, planted in 1896 and the 1930s, is visible from the trail, but it's not on the trail itself. Instead, almost all the trail's two-and-a-half-mile loop rolls through a deciduous forest of northern red oak, white oak, sugar maple, basswood, and wetland. A lattice of cross-country ski trails, groomed in the winter, intersects the Pine Knob Trail at several points, so you'll want to use the accompanying map to stay on course. The trail includes the longest, steepest ascent of any trail in the Abbey Arboretum. It skirts Mount Carmel ski hill, highest point in the arboretum, some 1,200 feet above sea level and once used for downhill skiing. It also passes

through an area of some 2,000 trees that blew down in about fifteen minutes in a severe windstorm in August 2011. Dr. Elizabeth Wurdak, professor of biology and one of this trail's regular walkers, says: "First I walk fast then gradually I slow down. I begin to notice the life around me, especially plants. I study them in detail and, as I do, my cares and stressful thoughts begin to fall away. New thoughts enter my mind. From them somehow emerge concrete plans for solving problems. Sometimes I catch sight of deer watching me from a distance, ready to bolt if I make a false move. I whisper to them my admiration for their grace and beauty. I feel refreshed and more confident when I return to the classroom and laboratory."

Begin just off the old entrance road, opposite the Old Stone Gate (above), designed and built by Father Joachim Watrin, O.S.B. (1906–1986), and a team of his confreres in 1931. Enter the clearing on the left side (north) of the road, where once stood

the Abbey's original sugar shack (1942), which burned down in 1970.

Father Sebastian Schramel, O.S.B. (1917–1999), with Father Fintan Bromenshenkel, O.S.B., helped build a new sugar shack closer to the sugar bush. Father Fintan (opposite) chopped and stacked wood in this clearing until he was more than ninety years old. It was his form of exercise, with summer garden work, to cure an ailing back.

Go right (northeast) past a ski trail path on your left that leads to Mount

Carmel. The Pine Knob Trail curves, gradually descends, and crosses between wetland. It rises and you pass a small boulder on the right, just before a road joins from the left. The trail then becomes more distinct. It passes a spur path back to the old entrance road, curves left (north), and gradually rises and falls. You'll walk past a large boulder on the left, then a stand of tall native oaks and maples (where the trail has a smooth cinder surface), pass another large boulder on the left, and head left (northwest) through a small open area. When you come to a juncture with a cross-country ski trail, which goes straight ahead, go left, through the area of the August 2011 blow down. Trees, unfortunately, are porous sound barriers, so you'll hear the hum of freeway traffic on your right. When Interstate 94 opened here in 1977 it sliced into eighty acres of Abbey land; the Abbey still owns another 400 acres on the other side of the interstate. The top of a large boulder protrudes from the forest floor just to the right of the trail.

You may see a spur path—called the "conifer cut-off"—on your left, a clearing on your right, and a northward connection to the boardwalk loop, also on your right. You'll pass a group of boulders on your left, and a small, flat clearing, with the prairie wetlands to your right in the distant north.

The trail rises with birch and red pine on the left and spruce, balsam fir, and a gully to the right. The Pine Knob Trail then comes to an intersection: the grassy boardwalk loop splits to the right, a logging road goes left. Go straight, past more pines and non-native brome grass on the left. The trail

curves southwest. You can see part of the oak savanna in the distance on your right. Sheep and cows once grazed in this area before the prairie was restored and the oak savanna was created in the late 1990s.

To stay on the Pine Knob Trail, leave the main road and follow the less-traveled dirt road southeast (or left) along the tree border; the radio tower is straight ahead. You're now at the southwest base of the Pine Knob, with its tall Scots pine and yellow pine high on the left. As you approach the gravel pit area, leave its road and go straight toward the trees. You'll see the northern end of the "conifer cut-off." From there, make a sharp turn right and follow the mown grass path west and south, looping around Cichy Pond below, beyond the trees on your left. The pond, named for Brother Elmer Cichy, O.S.B. (1915–2001), may once have drained into the watershed of the North Fork of the Watab River. There's a small spring that flows from a hill between Cichy Pond and East Gemini Lake.

The main dirt road, its gate, and the athletic fields come into view. Curve left along the elevated west shore of Cichy Pond, bordered by willows* and Scots pine. You can walk close to the outfield fence of the university baseball field or along a trail if it's mowed.

---

* In 2012 Saint John's hosted internationally known sculpture artist Patrick Dougherty for a residency to build on the prairie, east of County Road 159, a twenty-foot tall stickworks structure called *Lean on Me*, mostly from Salix willow branches harvested from the Abbey Arboretum (please see photo, p. 180).

If mown, follow the edge of the forest, with Durenberger Athletic Fields (named for Saint John's University's athletic director George Durenberger, 1907–1997) on the right. Skirting the fields and curving to the right, pass a well pump protected by a chain-link fence. Just before the baseball field's yellow foul poles align, follow the Pine Knob Trail back into the forest as it curves up to the right (west). On the left there's the outline of a path ascending south, once a toboggan run. Just before the asphalt road, follow the trail left (southeast). To the left is a network of cross-country ski trails. Follow the trail's long, steep ascent to the top of a rise, then a short descent, a brief ridge, and the trail curves southeast back to the start at Father Fintan's woodpile.

> The earth is the LORD's and all that is in it,
>   the world, and those who live in it;
> for he has founded it on the seas,
>   and established it on the rivers.
> Who shall ascend the hill of the LORD?
>   And who shall stand in his holy place?
>
> —Psalm 24:1-3

Vegetation of the Pine Knob

Leatherwood *Dirca palustris*

Shrub, grows up to ten feet, named for its tough bark. Twigs are so flexible they can be tied in knots without breaking. Leaves are inch and a half to three inches, egg shaped and smooth along the margins. Yellow flowers bloom early in the spring and develop into small green fruits.

Notable: Extremely shade tolerant, competes better than most shrubs in maple forests because it leafs out and flowers quickly in the spring. It won't be found in open forests or fire-prone landscapes; good indicator of a stable, mature forest.

At Saint John's

The seed dispersal system of the leatherwood plant is poorly understood. Biology professor Dr. Gordon Brown has done research with students on seed dispersal properties, hypothesizing that seed-caching rodents are an important piece of the puzzle.

Wild leek (or ramps) *Allium tricoccum*

A member of the lily family with broad leaves and parallel leaf venation. Ramps are among the first green plants on the forest floor in the spring, though their flowers won't emerge until midsummer when the leaves have dried up. Flowers are small, greenish-white, and arranged in an umbel (upside-down umbrella) at the end of the flowering stalk and developing into glossy black seeds in autumn. Found in moist, rich woods.

Notable: Another common name is "wild leek." Foliage has a strong garlic-onion aroma. Leaves and bulbs are edible and tasty when fried in butter or as a substitute for onions in any recipe.

At Saint John's

A patch of ramps grows in the woods near the Outdoor U offices. It is a common rite of spring to introduce student naturalists to this spring delicacy.

Red pine *Pinus resinosa*

Large, coniferous tree, grows to 120 feet. Bark is red-brown. Not all conifers are pines; in *true* pine trees, needles grow in bundles of two to five, while spruce and fir needles are attached to stems singly. Red pines have long, brittle needles in bundles of two.

Notable: Minnesota's state tree. The largest specimen in the world is in Itasca State Park, headwaters of the Mississippi River, 150 miles north of Saint John's.

At Saint John's

Michael Roske, manager of Abbey Woodworking, says the Abbey uses unstained red pine from the Abbey Arboretum for coffins for the Abbey's monks because of the wood's natural look and low cost. The monks once used basswood, stained black. Friends of Saint John's also can purchase coffins, created by Abbey Woodworking, in a variety of woods and stains.

Ironwood *Ostrya virginiana*

Small, shade-tolerant deciduous tree, commonly grows only thirty feet tall. Bark has brown-gray flat, scaly ridges. Named for its extremely dense wood. "Ostrya" is from the Greek (*ostrua*) for "bone-like." Leaves moderately hairy, with a dark green surface and pale green underside and teeth along the margins. Common in deciduous woodlands.

Notable: Another common name is hop hornbeam, referring to the fruits, which resemble hops (*Humulus lupulus*).

At Saint John's

One of the few species deer don't care to browse; it can grow into dense thickets in areas destined for oak regeneration and shade out young oaks. Prescribed burning sets it back significantly.

Lichens

Small moss-like organism growing on tree bark and stones. Over 700 species found in Minnesota. Lichens are understudied and often overlooked. These tiny organisms are communities of fungus and alga in a symbiotic relationship; the fungus creates the structure and the alga provides food through photosynthesis. Some species also include cyanobacteria. They vary from fiery yellow to drab gray, bright red to lime green. There are three main growth habits of lichens: crustose (looks like spray paint), foliose (grows flat like leaves), and fruticose (three-dimensional).

Notable: Certain species are sensitive to pollution, as they gather most nutrients from the air, rather than their host tree, rock, or ground. These lichens are bioindicators of air quality.

At Saint John's

Several species of common-tree lichens grow on rocks, trees, and the ground in the Abbey Arboretum, including white-wash lichen (looks like white chalk dust on maple bark), common green shield (seafoam-green foliose lichen), and powdered goldspeck (orange-yellow crustose lichen).

Blue stain fungus *Ceratocystis, Cholrociboria, and Ophiostoma fungal sp.* • *Year-round*

Have you ever stumbled on a fallen log that looks as if it were painted blue-green? One imagines forest gnomes with copper-blue paintbrushes, but this color is actually from any one of hundreds of fungi. The mycelium, or vegetative structure, spreads throughout the wood, dying it blue-green. Found on the forest floor of mixed woods.

Notable: Blue stain fungus is *saprophytic*, meaning it lives on decaying matter. But the blue stain fungus does not degrade the wood, only colors it as it feeds on the remaining sugars, not the cellulose wood fibers.

At Saint John's

Basswood and maple logs are especially susceptible to blue stain fungi. Logs from those species harvested at Saint John's each winter are cut to lumber and allowed to dry before June 1 to avoid the stain.

Turkey tail fungus *Trametes versicolor*
- *May–November, visible year-round*

This fan-shaped fungus ranges from one to four inches in size and resembles the flashy tail of a tom turkey.

Notable: The Latin *versicolor* is given to this fungus because of its variety of color: beige, brown, blue-green, and orange, ranging from dark to light.

At Saint John's

Many species of fungi display themselves in a moist, warm fall or spring, but turkey tails are most visible in the winter when leaves have fallen and snow gives a contrasting background.

Woodland sedges *Carex*

Low, tufted, grass-like plants. Leaves are green, but some species have purple, red, or yellow tints. There are 136 species of sedges in Minnesota. *Carex* and other grass-like plants are often overlooked; identification can be challenging.

Notable: Grasses, sedges, and rushes all have similar grass-like growth habits, with long and narrow leaves. Sedges are distinguished from the other two families by their triangular-shaped stems. Grasses have round, hollow stems and rushes have round, solid stems.

At Saint John's

When learning about sedges, grasses, and rushes, you can use this helpful rhyme to remember their distinguishing features: "Sedges have edges, rushes are round, grasses are hollow and grow from the ground."

Smooth sumac *Rhus glabra*

Large shrub, grows to twenty feet tall. Bark is gray, and young branches are smooth and green. Leaves are pinnately ("feather-shaped") and compound (several leaflets make up a single leaf), with nine to twenty-three serrated leaflets. Sumac has bright red fuzzy fruits, growing tightly in bunches, like grapes.

Notable: The fruits have a scent of lemon and can be steeped to make a citrus-flavored beverage reminiscent of lemonade once it is sweetened with sugar.

At Saint John's
Look for sumac along the Stumpf Lake bridge near the four-way stop as you enter the Saint John's campus; they turn brilliant scarlet in autumn.

Honeysuckle *Lonicera sp.*

Upright deciduous shrubs and vines. Leaves are simple, opposite, untoothed, and can be smooth or downy, depending on the species. Fragrant pink flowers in May and June produce bright red or yellow fruits that grow in pairs in the leaf axils. There are six native and three invasive honeysuckle species in Minnesota.

Notable: The exotic and invasive honeysuckles were introduced to North America as ornamental shrubs. They are difficult to control as many garden cultivars are still propagated by nurseries and birds spread the seeds. They can benefit wildlife, but exotic honeysuckles replace native forest shrubs and plants by their invasive nature and early leaf out.

At Saint John's

The most common honeysuckles at Saint John's are the three exotic ones, which are shrubs and can be distinguished from the native species by their hollow stems with a brown pith. Exotic honeysuckles are not considered as aggressive as European buckthorn, but they're more common at Saint John's than buckthorn.

> Then shall all the trees of the forest sing for joy
> before the LORD; for he is coming,
> for he is coming to judge the earth.
> He will judge the world with righteousness,
> and the peoples with his truth.
>
> —Psalm 96:12-13

Wildlife of the Pine Knob

Dung beetles *Coleoptera: Scarabaeoidae*

Stout, oval-shaped, a half-inch to an inch long. Vary from black to metallic blue-green or copper. The life cycle of a dung beetle depends on animal feces. Females deposit their eggs in a pile of dung and when the larvae hatch, they have plenty of nutritious food. Dung beetles have chewing mouthparts. Found in woodlands, grasslands, and farmland.

Notable: Related to the sacred Egyptian scarab beetles. They are harmless to humans and are good for ecosystems because they recycle excrement and eliminate habitat for filth-breeding flies.

At Saint John's

One of the most popular places on the boardwalk loop, where the trail is shared with the Pine Knob Trail, is the "bug dig," where we purposely put downed logs, rocks, and brush to create good insect habitat for children to explore.

Earthworms *Lumbricus sp.*

Vary from three to eight inches, light grey to reddish brown. Adult earthworms are distinguished from juveniles by a thick band around their middle called a clitellum, a reproductive organ. Earthworms also reproduce asexually when they are torn in half.

Notable: All species of earthworms in Minnesota are nonnative and are invasive. Earthworms are good for gardens but harm native forests. Fallen leaves naturally decompose slowly, forming the "duff layer" of spongy material where wildflower seeds germinate. Earthworms eat their way through all the duff each year, which invites other invasive species in, such as garlic mustard and buckthorn (which can grow in the compacted soil) and thins the herb layer of native wildflowers. Next time you go fishing, be sure to use up your worms and discard extra worms in the trash to help prevent the spread of these invasive invertebrates. Beware of buying worms for composting. The chance of them escaping is not worth the compost.

At Saint John's

Seventh graders on Outdoor U field trips study the effects of invasive earthworms on forest habitat. After dissolving a cup of ground mustard in a gallon of water and slowly pouring it into the ground, the students count the earthworms that surface after being irritated by the solution. During wet seasons, some students have counted more than one hundred worms in a square meter of ground.

Flying squirrel *Glaucomys volans* • *Year-round*

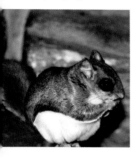

Smaller than the eastern chipmunk, with large eyes, brownish-gray fur on the back and a white belly. They are nocturnal rodents, feeding on acorns, other seeds, buds, insects, and the occasional songbird. Sometimes at night, flying squirrels will visit bird feeders for seed. They sleep in dens together in the winter but are not true hibernators.

Notable: Flying squirrels don't fly. They glide, using their flat tail and patagium (a fold of skin connecting the front and back legs) to escape danger or cover distances quickly. They typically glide for twenty to thirty feet but are known to "fly" as far as 150 feet.

At Saint John's

Biology professor Kristina Timmerman has led field research to study the population of flying squirrels in the Abbey Arboretum since 2012. She and her students have trapped and tagged squirrels, and they estimate a healthy population of 2.52 squirrels per acre. They continue studies to gain a deeper understanding of the species.

Raccoon *Procyon lotor* • *Spring–Fall*

Medium-sized omnivorous mammal, fifteen to thirty inches long. Distinctive black "mask" and ringed tail. Raccoons are great climbers but most often find food on the ground. Diet includes crayfish, grasshoppers, fish, turtles, birds, voles, mice, fruits, squirrel, acorns, and grains. Primarily nocturnal. Dens underground, in abandoned buildings, haystacks, and snowdrifts.

Notable: Cousins to the bear family. Raccoons are often considered a pest or a nuisance, but you can use a tight-fitting lid on your garbage can or an electric fence around your garden to help keep them out.

At Saint John's
It is not uncommon for young raccoons to be found huddling in the "honeycomb" windows of the Peter Engel Science Center, or even napping in a dumpster on campus.

Boreal chorus frog *Pseudacris triseriata*

Small, slender, three-fourths of an inch to an inch-and-a-half long. Varies from tan to gray, red, or green, but distinguished by a dark stripe through the eye, a white line along the upper lip, and three dark lines along the back. Chorus frogs eat spiders, ants, beetles, and other small insects. Found in forest ponds.

Notable: The call of a chorus frog is like a fingernail clicking across the teeth of a comb.

In spring, snowmelt pools in low spots of the hardwood forest to form seasonal ponds where insects and frogs congregate.

Barred owl *Strix varia* • *Year-round*

Stocky, with a round head and rounded tail; twenty to twenty-one inches tall. Brown and white vertical streaking on belly; mostly brown on back. Large brown eyes, no ear tufts. Barred owls have a recognizable hoot, remembered with the phrase, "Who cooks for you, who cooks for you all?" Fairly common in woodlands.

Notable: A barred owl's right ear is higher than its left ear. Hearing from two different angles helps it pinpoint its prey.

At Saint John's
Outdoor U hosts an "Owl Hoot" every February, to familiarize guests with the twelve owl species found in Minnesota and how they survive year-round.

White-breasted nuthatch *Sitta carolinensis* • *Year-round*

Small songbird with a short tail and large head; five and three-fourths inches tall. Males have a black cap; females, dark blue-gray. Both have a blue-gray back, white breast, long, skinny black beak and black eye. The feathers on the lower belly and under the tail are chestnut. Nuthatches usually perch upside down on trees. Its call, though, is hardly a song but more of a nasal, monotonous *yank-yank-yank-yank*. Common in deciduous woodlands and at home feeders.

Notable: These clever birds get the name "nuthatch" because they jam acorns and other large nuts into the bark of trees, then poke the seeds out using their sharp beaks.

At Saint John's
Because of its perching habits and easy-to-remember call, the nuthatch or "upside-down bird" is an easy species for children and novice birders to identify.

Wild turkey *Meleagris gallopavo* • *Year-round*

Plump, chicken-like bird with long neck and small head. Males forty-eight inches tall, females thirty-six inches. Dark overall, with bronze-green iridescent feathers. Wing feathers have white bars; tail feathers are broad with rusty tips. The male turkey has a bluish, featherless head, red wattles, and a beard of feathers on breast. The female bird is smaller with muted colors; usually beardless. The male's call is a familiar gobble, like the domesticated species. Found in open forests and clearings, often in flocks. They love acorns.

Notable: Since they're such heavy birds, turkeys are more likely to run than fly when threatened.

At Saint John's
In October 1996 Father Don Talafous, O.S.B., alumni chaplain for Saint John's University, encountered two wild turkeys on one of his hikes to Stella Maris Chapel. "Halfway over I saw a student, a runner, standing with two wild turkeys,

apparently trying to quell their zealous attention to him. They offered me some of the same but I managed to continue out to the chapel. Leaving the chapel for the return trip, I decided it might be good to pick up a hefty tree branch in case I met the unwelcome attentions of the same turkeys. Sure enough, they were waiting for me. They nipped and pecked at me somewhat like a couple of unfriendly dogs. I tried to fend [them] off for what would amount to a city block. All this time I was walking, nearly running, backwards. Finally they gave up the chase."

Pileated woodpecker *Dryocopus pileatus* • *Year-round*

Large, crow-sized woodpecker, sixteen to seventeen inches tall, found in woodlands. Black with a striking red crest and white stripes on the neck. The male has a flashy red mustache. Pileated woodpeckers often can be heard drumming, as they excavate trees, searching for carpenter ants. They leave large, rectangular holes that can be a foot or more long. All woodpeckers have an undulating flight pattern that helps to distinguish them from other birds.

Notable: The pileated woodpecker's call is a loud, fast, high-pitched laughing sound, like a monkey's howl. The large cavities they excavate in trees provide nesting spots for other birds from bluebirds to barred owls.

At Saint John's

Other woodpeckers commonly found at the Abbey Arboretum are the downy woodpecker (*picoides pubescens*), hairy woodpecker (*picoides villosus*), red-bellied woodpecker (*melanerpes carolinus*), and northern flicker (*colaptes auratus*).

> And God said, "Let the waters bring forth swarms of living creatures, and let birds fly above the earth across the dome of the sky." So God created the great sea monsters and every living creature that moves, of every kind, with which the waters swarm, and every winged bird of every kind. And God saw that it was good.
>
> —Genesis 1:20-21

Eastern bluebird *Sialia sialis*

A blue- and rusty-colored songbird found throughout Minnesota, especially in areas with a mix of woodlands and grass. Bluebirds nest from late March through early August, building cup-like nests of grass or pine needles in a nest box or other cavity.

Notable: Bluebirds are a symbol of happiness and are considered by some to be Minnesota's most popular songbird. Bluebirds declined greatly in the mid-1900s due to competition from other cavity-nesting birds, especially starlings and house sparrows. Minnesota now has one of the most successful bluebird recovery projects in the nation, led by the construction and maintenance of bluebird boxes that are not subject to predation.

At Saint John's

Beginning in 1985, Father Bruce Wollmering, O.S.B. (1940–2009), created a trail of some seventy nesting boxes for eastern bluebirds throughout the Abbey Arboretum, including parts of the Pine Knob Trail. Volunteers monitor the boxes weekly from mid-March through mid-September to track nests, eggs, babies, and fledglings. The data are reported to the Minnesota Bluebird Recovery Program, often reporting seventy to one hundred fledglings annually.

Cross-Country Skiing

Some consider Minnesota's long, snowy winters a burden, but it's really a great time to be outdoors and explore nature. Without leaves, the shape of the hills is more visible than in summer, and each species of a tree can be identified by its bark or crown growth. Animal tracks show clearly in the snow and can be followed for miles. Brother Lew Grobe, O.S.B., said he didn't fully appreciate the topography of Saint John's until he cross-country skied the trails, that "the constant rise and fall of the trails gives one a better sense of the ruggedness of the land. I discovered many ponds and marshes hidden by summer vegetation." His fellow skier, Father Nickolas Kleespie, O.S.B., who

also swims, bikes, and runs, finds skiing helps him connect spiritually to the land throughout the long winter.

The Abbey Arboretum grooms about twenty kilometers (12.4 miles) of trails for classic and skate skiing. The Stone Gate Loop Trail is gentle, welcoming to novices, and brings you into an area of oak, maple, and basswood that casual visitors don't often see. The Pine Knob Trail is of medium difficulty, through mostly deciduous forest, but passes through glades of pine trees planted by early monks. Most difficult of all is the Trinity Loop, a series of trails within the Pine Knob Trail with steep slopes and sharp turns. David Johnson, an exercise physiologist and coach of the CSB/SJU Nordic ski team from 2000 to 2011, planned the cross-country ski trails in 2000, to follow, as he wrote, "the natural lay of the land . . . where erosion from foot traffic and water runoff is minimal."

If you must walk on the groomed ski trails, please walk on the edge of the ski trail opposite the classical track. All other ungroomed trails in the woods are perfect for winter walks and snowshoeing.

The Climate of Saint John's: A "Theoretical Happy Medium"

Saint John's is 1,200 feet above sea level in the North Temperate Zone, latitude 45 degrees 36', halfway between the equator and north pole, a "theoretical happy medium," as two monks rosily put it in 1945. It's also in Zone 4b of the US Department of Agriculture's plant hardiness eleven-zone map, which gardeners and growers use to determine plants most likely to thrive in a location; 4a has an average annual low temperature of twenty-five to thirty degrees below zero Fahrenheit. The growing season of Saint John's is late May to mid-September, when the climate generally is humid from spring through early fall, with usually dependable summer rains.

The University's weather station, on the roof of the Peter Engel Science Center, is a solar-powered Davis Wireless Vantage Pro2 Plus 6163. It updates data every two-and-a-half seconds with an anemometer (wind speed), thermo-hygro sensor (temperature-humidity), solar sensor, and rain gauge. (Current readings: weatherstation.csbsju.edu.) The building and the weather station are named after Saint John's fourth abbot, Father Peter Engel, O.S.B. (1856–1921), who began recording data for the US Weather Bureau on October 12, 1892, to celebrate the 400th anniversary of Columbus's discovery of America. On that day, thirty-four-year-old Abbot Peter climbed the five-story staircase to the southeast turret of the Quadrangle and, at 8:30 a.m., looked out over the forest and lakes of Saint John's and wrote in pencil on his US Army Signal Service form:

Temperature	59°F
Barometric pressure	29.960
Dew point	43
Relative Humidity	54
Wind	SE
Precipitation	0
Sky	Cloudy

A professor of natural philosophy, physics, and chemistry, ornithologist in his private time, and abbot for a quarter century, he was a deeply spiritual man who embraced science and technology, confident that scientific progress showed the hand of God. His creation of a photography studio is the primary reason Saint John's has such a rich visual history. One of his favorite phrases was the Latin *crescat, crescant* (may it grow). To his confreres who might object to his latest innovation he would reply, "Well, we must be up with the times, Father." His study of climate and meteorology grew from his love of astronomy. He designed the Abbey's brick observatory (1894–1961), built on high ground where the prep school now overlooks Lake Sagatagan. Father Melchior Freund, O.S.B. (1930–2005), astronomer, teacher, and meteorologist, served as Saint John's weather recorder for the National Weather Service from 1951 to 1957 and from 1968 to 2004. There was, for Father "Mel," a practical link between the stars and the earth. "Astronomy is a science that gains respect when we are able to think beyond practicality," he wrote. "Just knowing how vast and how alive the universe is and our comparative smallness seems infinitely practical to me."

Lake Sagatagan latest ice out	May 7, 2013
Average annual rainfall	28.7 inches
Average annual snowfall	50.4 inches
Highest temperature	+106°F, July 10, 1936
Lowest temperature	-39°F, January 22, 1936
Minnesota's greatest monthly snowfall	66.4 inches (Collegeville, March 1965)
Winter 1964–65 snowfall	109.2 inches
March 17, 1965, snow depth	41 inches
Single storm record snowfall	26.6 inches, November 10–12, 1940 (Armistice Day Blizzard)

Sources: ncdc.noaa.org; Mark W. Seeley, *Minnesota Weather Almanac*. Minnesota Historical Society, 2006.

"Collegeville also holds two state records for total daily precipitation: 1.75 inches on February 9, 1909 (the liquid equivalent of a 14-inch snowfall), and 5.84 inches . . . on May 22, 1962. Collegeville's monthly record for total rainfall, 15.16 inches, set in July 1913, is one of the state's highest as well. With its elevation of 1,242 feet above mean sea level, Collegeville sits relatively higher than most of the central Minnesota landscape, [which] may contribute to its larger precipitation totals." Mark W. Seeley

The Northern Lights:
"An Immense, Luminous Tent"

Our northern sky is an intimate part of the Abbey Arboretum, perfect for stargazing and cloud gazing. It's seldom more dramatic than during an appearance of the aurora borealis, the so-called northern lights, when highly charged electrons from solar wind interact with elements in the earth's magnetic atmosphere. Brother Bruno Doerfler, O.S.B., left this description of an aurora borealis on Sunday night, July 17, 1892. His pen and paper were almost as good as a camera, his words have the flavor of the book of Revelation:

The Aurora was first noticed at 8:55 p.m. It was then very faint but increased continually in brightness until about 9:30, when it had obtained a Zenith Distance of about 45 degrees and extended along the northern horizon for a distance of about 150 degrees. . . . A beautiful sunset tinge travelled from east to west in large patches, some of them 25 to 30 degrees in diameter. Beautiful greenish and bluish streamers shot up from the horizon in every direction with enormous speed, some reaching the Zenith in 5 to 10 seconds. These streamers also travelled from east to west at the rate of 30 to 40 degrees per minute. At the same time a band of electric light about 5 degrees wide extended along the whole Ecliptic. These phenomena continued to become more intense until 9:40, when they attained their maximum. . . . Beautiful roseate streamers shot up to a Zenith Distance of about 30 degrees in every direction while yellowish, bluish and greenish streamers, rising along the whole horizon. . . . This gave to the sky an appearance of the interior of an immense, luminous tent . . . the surrounding country was so illuminated that farm buildings could be seen at a distance of 3 or 4 miles. It was certainly light enough to read ordinary newspaper print outside. . . . This aurora was by far the finest one ever observed by the writer. At 9:50 p.m. a meteor having nearly the brightness of Venus at her best was seen falling from a point on the meridian about 40 degrees from the Zenith. It fell towards the east, its path making an angle of about 40 degrees with the horizon. It travelled a distance of about 30 degrees, occupying about 5 seconds in its passage. The trail remained visible to the naked eye for about three seconds.

O Lord, our Sovereign,
    how majestic is your name in all the earth!
You have set your glory above the heavens.

—Psalm 8:1

The Gift of the Abbey Arboretum

When the land does well for its owner, and the owner does well by his land; when both end up better by reason of their partnership, we have conservation.

—Aldo Leopold, Conservationist

The Benedictine monks of Saint John's have always been conservationists at heart. They look generations ahead with a true faith that their work, as a complement to worship, will be rewarded. When they first laid claim to this land in the mid-nineteenth century, they set about to steward its bounty to sustain both the environment and its human inhabitants. The 1,500-year-old *Rule of Benedict* directed them to "regard all the utensils of the monastery and its whole property as if they were the sacred vessels of the altar." By respecting all the wonder flowing from God, the land and people thrived.

In 1997, the Benedictines officially designated these nurtured woods, lakes, ponds, and prairies as an *Arboretum*—a large, naturally functioning ecosystem to be protected and managed as a place to work, discover, and educate. Today we still manage the land using both Benedictine principles and *Benedictine time*. A tree may take 150 years to grow from acorn to towering oak, the equivalent of six human generations. We plant, nurture, and harvest the forests with this in mind.

Saint John's has embraced current forestry trends such as mechanizing timber-harvesting equipment (trees are no longer cut, thankfully, using spit and a crosscut saw) and computerized data mapping. Our forest data and maps, updated by students learning geographic information systems, enable us to identify and track forest growth down to the acre—unimaginably more sophisticated than the hand-drawn maps that Gifford Pinchot used when he helped create the US Forest Service for President Theodore Roosevelt in 1905. Incidentally, that was more than a decade after our Father Adrian Schmitt, O.S.B., was practicing forestry here.

The thoughtful regeneration of high-quality hardwoods such as oak is a Saint John's priority. We still use red and white oak trees to build the sturdy desks and chairs you see about campus. Oak also provides mast, or acorns, to sustain deer, squirrels, and other animals. The Benedictines plant and leave enough trees to seed the ground so that the land continues to provide. It's no surprise that the Minnesota Department of Natural Resources designates most of Saint John's oak and maple-basswood forests as *sites of outstanding biological significance.*

No one can predict what's ahead for forests over the next 150 years. One trend, however, already is clear. With continued population growth and expanding urban areas, natural preserves such as the Saint John's Abbey Arboretum are becoming even more scarce and more critical as intact ecological spaces. We fervently pray that this sacred vessel of nature—which the Benedictines have so thoughtfully protected and perpetuated for more than a century and a half—will remain a model of conservation for centuries to come.

Thomas Kroll
Land Manager, Saint John's Abbey
  Arboretum
Director, Saint John's Outdoor
  University

The sun was trembling now on the edge of the ridge. It was alive, almost fluid and pulsating, and as I watched it sink I thought that I could feel the earth turning from it, actually feel its rotation. Over all was the silence of the wilderness, that sense of oneness which comes only when there are no distracting sights or sounds, when we listen with inward ears and see with inward eyes, when we feel and are aware with our entire beings rather than our senses. I thought as I sat there of the ancient admonition "Be still and know that I am God," and knew that without stillness there can be no knowing, without divorcement from outside influences man cannot know what spirit means.

—Sigurd F. Olson (1899–1982),
  Singing Wilderness (1956)

A Chronology
of Benedictine
Stewardship

480–547   Benedict of Nursia, founder of what became the Order of
          Saint Benedict and Western monasticism

777   Tassilo III, duke of Bavaria, founds the Benedictine monastery
          of Kremsmünster Abbey in Upper Austria; its forest still has a
          rotation length over two hundred years in the upper mountains

1856   Benedictine monks come to the Minnesota Territory with
          tree seeds in their pockets; cut tamarack logs and gather
          fieldstone for first monastic homestead; hundreds of cords
          later used to heat the Quadrangle

1868   First bricks made from Saint John's clay for Abbey buildings

1872   Stella Maris ("Star of the Sea") Chapel built on Lake Sagata-
          gan to honor Mary, the Mother of God

1892   Monks create trail to Stella Maris Chapel (accessible previ-
          ously only by boat)

1894   Evening of June 27 a tornado damages or destroys many
          buildings and trees

1896   First conifer plantation at Saint John's, re-creating Bavarian
          forests (today 130 acres of conifers): Scots, red pine, and

Norway spruce planted south of what is now the Saint John's Prep campus on Pickerel Point

1900 James Katzner, O.S.B., begins planting several thousand evergreens on campus

1903 April 17: Lightning strike starts fire that destroys Stella Maris Chapel

1906 Monks plant Scots pines (the Swayed Pines) on what today is western entry to the Clemens football stadium

1915 Monks build current Stella Maris Chapel

1926 Alexius Hoffmann, O.S.B., begins compiling "Natural History of Collegeville," first major effort to document plants, animals, and geology of Saint John's (completed 1934)

1933 July 22: Abbot Alcuin Deutsch, O.S.B., signs contract setting aside Saint John's Abbey's then-2,438 acres as a state wildlife refuge (prohibits carrying of firearms and taking of game birds by other than trapping or snaring); Father Angelo Zankl, O.S.B., named Collegeville's first game warden

1935 Five tame deer introduced

1942 First record of Saint John's sugar bush maple syrup harvest

1949 Abbey sets aside 160 acres of forest around Lake Sagatagan and 400 acres of lakes and swamp as "areas to be preserved," no harvesting of trees allowed

1961 *Cornus alternifolia*, Pagoda dogwood, planted in west cloister garden of Abbey and University Church

1966 Dam built to create East Gemini Lake, receiving phosphorus from wastewater treatment

1980 *Magnolia stellata* planted in Quadrangle courtyard (oldest magnolia on campus), blossomed every year since

1980s Master Plan proposes planting lines of trees along major trails and roads of inner campus, including native trees for major plantings and exotics for interest, including basswoods accented by redbuds, hawthorns, cork trees, dogwoods, forsythia shrubs to highlight native leatherwoods

1984   Father Paul Schwietz, O.S.B., envisions natural arboretum for Saint John's as "part of a worshipping community rooted in place"; later, on European sabbatical, inspired by monasteries connected with their forests

1986   First controlled burn of oak savanna; Father Paul Schwietz, O.S.B., and Mike Maurer and Fred Bengston of the Minnesota Department of Natural Resources, conceive a Habitat Restoration Project (HRP), to restore more diversity to the landscape after more than a century of farming and fallow ground

1988   Two earthen dams built to hold back water as part of Habitat Restoration Project (HRP) to restore sixty acres of wetlands once farmed for meadow hay; savanna restoration begins with securing firebreaks and planned burning to eliminate pioneer trees; savanna had been pasture, then fallow for almost thirty years

1988   Rows of white oaks planted near auditorium and church plaza, and a bosquet of linden in the auditorium plaza

1991   As part of HRP, about ninety species of prairie grasses and flowers (4,800 plants) planted to restore tall-grass, wet and dry prairie on fifty acres where crops had grown

1993   Saint John's University adopts environmental studies as an academic minor

1995   Saint John's adopts three-year cycle of planned burns to save HRP habitat for birds and insects; last time Saint John's prairie is burned in its entirety

1996-97   More than one hundred dead deer found during two winters, result of deer overpopulation

1997   Saint John's designates and dedicates natural arboretum; forty-five deer are "harvested" including forty does (deer browse replanted herbaceous plants such as flowers, sedges, and grasses that reduce insect and bird populations that depend on those plants); Saint John's completes inventory of arboretum's vegetation to improve the land's natural diversity

1998   Summer inventory of prairie and upper part of wetlands reveals more than one hundred prairie species; 100,000 board feet harvested from about 1,300 acres; double row of red oaks planted along campus main entrance road

1999   Flowering crabs planted at campus entry circle

2000   May 4: Father Paul Schwietz, O.S.B., dies of heart failure; John Geissler named acting director

2001   Veteran forester Tom Kroll named head of Saint John's Abbey Arboretum

2001   Eighty-plus species of native grass and flowers reintroduced on another five acres of HRP oak savanna; two boardwalks spanning 1,350 feet installed to provide for loop trail, led by John Geissler

2002   Survey of Lake Hilary, led by biology professor Dr. Gordon Brown, finds ancient pollen of white, jack, and Norway pine, black spruce; Saint John's University and College of Saint Benedict create environmental studies major; Forest Stewardship Council certifies Saint John's Abbey Arboretum as "well-managed" under its Smartwood audit, verifying that Saint John's grows and harvests its trees sustainably

2003   Saint John's Abbey, with gift from anonymous donor, purchases one hundred acres of farmland west of West Gemini Lake from the Philippi family to help preserve rural character of the landscape as part of the "Avon Hills Conservation Plan"

2008   Prairie plant seeds dispersed on twelve acres overlooking West Gemini Lake; forty-four species of flowering herbs (forbs) and oats seeded to compete against common garden weeds such as pigweed and lamb's-quarter

2010   US Geological Survey captures loons at Saint John's to take measurements, blood samples, and surgically implant satellite transmitters to track their migration patterns

2011 August 2 storm at 8:00 a.m. blows down some 2,000 trees in fifteen minutes; salvage harvest continues for three years

2012 Saint John's Arboretum divides into two entities, reflecting growth in its programs and the Abbey's land steward-ship. The first entity—the 2,500 acres of lakes, prairie, oak savanna, and forest, owned by Saint John's Abbey and sur-rounding Saint John's University—becomes known as Saint John's Abbey Arboretum.

2013 The second entity, for Arboretum programming, is named Saint John's Outdoor University. It provides outdoor and environmental education with the Abbey Arboretum, Saint John's University, and the College of Saint Benedict.

Nineteen acres of oak planted for regeneration; deer ex-clusion zone created by Brother Walter Kieffer, O.S.B., and Americorps-National Civilian work crew.

Consider the lilies, how they grow: they neither toil nor spin; yet I tell you, even Solomon in all his glory was not clothed like one of these.

—Luke 12:27

Sources*

Arden, John. "Saint John's Cuts Trees So Forest May Thrive." *The Record* (March 1, 1974): 3.

Barry, Colman, O.S.B. *Worship and Work: Saint John's Abbey and University, 1856–1980*. Collegeville, MN: Saint John's Abbey, 1980.

Bauer, Nancy, O.S.B. "Sister Remberta Westkaemper, O.S.B.: Finding God in the Forest." Conference presentation. November 4, 2006.

Brenny, Christopher. "Pest on the Prairie: Absinth Wormwood." *Sagatagan Seasons* 8, no. 3 (Summer 2005): 2.

Britz, Jennifer Delahunty. "Evergreen!" *Saint John's* magazine (Winter 2003).

Brogan, Grace. "Is the Answer Blowing in the Wind?" *Sagatagan Seasons* 8, no. 2 (Spring 2005): 1, 6.

———. "Saint John's Historic Pine Curtain." *Sagatagan Seasons* 7, no. 1 (Winter 2004): 2.

———. "Saint John's 'Pine Curtain.' " *The Abbey Banner* (Winter 2003): 4–5.

Bromenshenkl, Sylvan, and Roman Schneider. "Our Weather and Climate." *The Scriptorium* 2 (Summer 1945): 40–49.

"Brother Ansgar Is Active in Forestry." *The Record* (May 13, 1926): 5.

"Brother Ansgar Directs the Annual Reforestation." *The Record* (May 5, 1927): 7.

Brown, Brian C. "In My Own Backyard." *Sagatagan Seasons* 5, no. 2 (Summer 2002): 2.

* You can find most of the listed sources at the SJU Archives online (csbsju .edu/sju-archives).

Coudron, Curt. "Featured Arboretum Connection: Father Gunther Rolfson, O.S.B." *Sagatagan Seasons* 3, no. 4 (Winter 2000): 3.

Davis, Larry E. "Stone Walls: Stories from Minnesota's Geologic Past." *Headwaters: The Faculty Journal of the College of Saint Benedict and Saint John's University* 24 (2007): 4–16.

Davisson, Allan. "Clustering and Overlays: Keys to Avon Hills Protection." *Sagatagan Seasons* 8, no. 4 (Fall 2005): 2, 6.

Delfs, Katelynne. "Choose Your Own Adventure." *Sagatagan Seasons* 15, no. 3 (Summer 2012): 4–5.

Deutsch, Alfred. "*Ding an sich* or Watab Bottoms." *Abbey Quarterly* 2, no. 1 (January 1984): 6–7.

———. "Editor's Farewell: To Autumn." *Abbey Quarterly* 7, no. 4 (October 1989): 5.

———. "Father Paul Outlines Care for Abbey Woods and Lakes." *Abbey Quarterly* 5, no. 1 (January 1987): 6–7.

———. "Gardens and Gardeners: Harvest Time at Saint John's Abbey." *Abbey Quarterly* 5, no. 4 (October 1987): 6–7.

———, ed. "Saint John's Furniture, 1874–1974." Unpublished manuscript, 1974.

———. "Stone Walls: A Forgotten Tradition." *Abbey Quarterly* 1, no. 4 (October 1983): 7.

———. "Watercress and the Hazards of Home Brew." *Abbey Quarterly* 2, no. 4 (October 1984): 2.

Doerfler, Bruno. "Aurora Borealis." July 17, 1892. Saint John's Abbey Archives.

Evanson, Alex. "Father Angelo Zankl: Saint John's Volume of Living History." *Sagatagan Seasons* 2, no. 2 (Spring 1999): insert.

"Father John Produces Remarkable Pear Crop." *The Record* (September 23, 1926): 1.

Francis, Pope. *Laudato Sì* (On Care for Our Common Home). Encyclical Letter. May 24, 2015.

Franklin, Emily. "First Game Warden at Saint John's Abbey: Father Angelo Zankl." *Sagatagan Seasons* 8, no. 4 (Fall 2005).

———. "Spring Thaw on the Prairie." *Sagatagan Seasons* 9, no. 2 (Spring 2006): 1, 6.

Geissler, John. "Spring's Sweet Flow." *Sagatagan Seasons* 6, no. 1 (Spring 2003): 1.

Gray, Eleanor. "From Acorn to Chair—A Life Cycle of Saint John's Abbey Wood." *Sagatagan Seasons* 16, no. 1 (Winter 2013): 4–5.

———. "A Storied Trail." *Sagatagan Seasons* 15, no. 3 (Summer 2012): 1–2.

Guza, Becky. "Arboretum Plant of the Month: Leadplant." *Sagatagan Seasons* 4, no. 2 (Summer 2001): 3.

Halbur, Adam. "Prairie and Oak Savanna Burns." *Sagatagan Seasons* 1, no. 2 (Spring 1998): 3.

Hansen, Henry L., and Lawrence B. Ritter. "Saint John's Forest Plantations." *Minnesota Department of Conservation* magazine (May–June 1951): 28–30.

Hansen, Steve. "The Watershed of Saint John's: A New Sense of Place." *Sagatagan Seasons* 6, no. 1 (Spring 2003): 4–5.

Hanson, John. "Astronomy at Saint John's." *Abbey Quarterly* (Fall 1994): 6, 8.

Healy, Luke. "Red-Shouldered Hawk." *Sagatagan Seasons* 4, no. 2 (Summer 2001): 5.

Herbst, Cassie. "Dragonflies of Minnesota." *Sagatagan Seasons* 11, no. 1 (Winter 2008): 1, 6.

———. "How's the Weather in Your Neck of the Woods?" *Sagatagan Seasons* 12, no. 2 (Spring 2009): 3.

Hoffmann, Alexius. "Natural History of Collegeville, Minnesota." Unpublished manuscript, 1934.

———. "The Vision of the Island." *The Record* (1896): 140–43.

Holmen, R. W. "Spirit of a Liberal" (blog). *DonGeng*, January 16, 2014, http://www.theliberalspirit.com.

Hughes, Kathleen. *The Monk's Tale: A Biography of Godfrey Diekmann, O.S.B.* Collegeville, MN: Liturgical Press, 1991.

Johnson, David A. "Saint John's Arboretum Cross-Country Ski Trails." *Sagatagan Seasons* 7, no. 1 (Winter 2004): 7.

Kroll, Mary. "In The Beginning . . ." *Sagatagan Seasons* 10, no. 2 (Spring 2007): 1, 6.

Kroll, Thomas. "Director's Notes." *Sagatagan Seasons* 5, no. 1 (Spring 2002): 8.

————. "What's in a Name." *Sagatagan Seasons* 16, no. 2 (Spring 2013): 1–2.

Kulas, John. "The Abbey and Its Land." *Sagatagan Seasons* 10, no. 2 (Spring 2007): 4, 6.

Kutter, Jenny. "Hollow in There!" *Sagatagan Seasons* 16, no. 4 (Autumn 2013): 1–2.

————. "In Memory of Father Bruce Wollmering, O.S.B." *Sagatagan Seasons* 12, no. 2 (Spring 2009): 6.

————. "In Memory of Father James Tingerthal." *Sagatagan Seasons* 12, no. 4 (Autumn 2009): 6.

————. "Managing Tomorrow's Trees." *Sagatagan Seasons* 11, no. 4 (Autumn 2008): 3, 6.

Kutter, Ryan. "Bringing the Word to Life." *Sagatagan Seasons* 8, no. 1 (Winter 2005): 1, 6.

Lyndgaard, Kyhl. "Never the Same Trail Twice." *Sagatagan Seasons* 7, no. 4 (Autumn 2004): 3, 7.

Maric, Marina. "The Joys of Collecting Sap (and Plums!)." *Sagatagan Seasons* 7, no. 3 (Summer 2004): 2.

Meinberg, Father Clodoald, O.S.B. "Sagatagan Saga." *The Scriptorium* (Summer 1945): 25–38.

Melchoir, Paul, and Stephen G. Saupe. "The Floral Charms of Saint John's: A Survey of Botanical Communities." Unpublished manuscript, 2007.

Meyer, Jeffrey. "A Short History of Farming at Saint John's." Unpublished manuscript, 1975. Saint John's Abbey Archives.

Minnesota Land Trust (www.mnland.org/about).

Murphy, Nora. "The Maples: Is This Land My Land?" In *The State We're In: Reflections on Minnesota History.* Edited by Annette Atkins and Deborah L. Miller. Saint Paul: Minnesota Historical Society, 2010.

Poff, Jim. "The Dragonflies of Collegeville."

Reimer, Emily. "A Loop for Kids of All Ages." *Sagatagan Seasons* 15, no. 3 (Summer 2012): 3.

Reinhart, Dietrich. "A History of the Saint John's Carpentry Shop." In "Saint John's Furniture, 1874–1974," 8–12. Edited by Alfred Deutsch. 1974.

Robbins, Will. "Footprints from the Past." *Sagatagan Seasons* 9, no. 1 (Winter 2006): 2, 6.

Robertson, Colin. "Maple Syrup Soon!" *Sagatagan Seasons* 2, no. 1 (Winter 1999), 3.

———. "Plant of the Season: Eastern White Pine Pinus Strobus." *Sagatagan Seasons* 2, no. 1 (Winter 1999): 3–4.

Rolfson, Gunther. "Our Scientific Endeavor." *The Scriptorium* 2 (Summer 1945): 18–24.

Roske, Peggy. "History of the Land of Saint John's Abbey." Presentation to the Avon Hills Conference. Saint John's University, Collegeville, MN, February 1, 2014.

Russell, Robert. "Movements of the Windbirds." *Sagatagan Seasons* 6, no. 3 (Autumn 2003): 2.

"Saint John's [Forestry] Activities Featured by Paper." *The Record* (May 23, 1929): 1, 9.

Santich, Jan Joseph (Benedict). "Sagatagan Names." *The Scriptorium* 25 (December 1986): vii–x.

———. "A Tiny Warbler in a Big World." *Sagatagan Seasons* 16, no. 2 (Spring 2013): 2–3.

Saupe, Stephen G. "The Bailey Herbarium." *Sagatagan Seasons* 2, no. 4 (Winter 2000): 1.

———. "European Buckthorn Is My Favorite Plant—Not!" *Sagatagan Seasons* 6, no. 3 (Autumn 2003).

———. "A Fine Lady and Excellent Field Botanist: Sister Remberta Westkaemper, O.S.B." February 5, 2015.

———. "The Maple Syrup 'Crystal Ball.'" *Sagatagan Seasons* 8, no. 2 (Spring 2005): 4.

———. "Maple Syrup: Saint John's Sweetest Springtime Tradition." Unpublished manuscript, 2006.

———. "Maple Syruping and the Weather." *Sagatagan Seasons* 12, no. 2 (Spring 2009): 1–2.

———. "The Space Age Sugar Shack." *Sagatagan Seasons* 16, no. 2 (Spring 2013): 5.

Schmidt, Andy. "Restoration with Fire." *Sagatagan Seasons* 3, no. 1 (Spring 2000): 2.

Schwietz, Paul. "Benedictine Principles: An Ecological Approach." *Sagatagan Seasons* 15, no. 1 (Winter 2012): 3.

———. "Benedictine Stewardship—An Ecological Approach." *Sagatagan Seasons* 2, no. 1 (Winter 1999): 2.

———. "Notes from the Director." *Sagatagan Seasons* 2, no. 1 (Winter 1999): 1, 4.

———. "Restoration: a Key Principle of the Arboretum's Mission." *Sagatagan Seasons* 2, no. 3 (Summer 1999): 4.

Sieh, Bryan. "Some Say the Arboretum Is Loony." *Sagatagan Seasons* 13, no. 4 (Autumn 2010): 6.

Sim, Elizabeth. "Avon Hills: Planning for the Future." *Sagatagan Seasons* 6, no. 3 (Autumn 2003): 4, 6.

———. "Invasion of the Alien Earthworms." *Sagatagan Seasons* 6, no. 2 (Summer 2003): 1, 6.

———. "New Land Preserves Saint John's Viewshed." *Sagatagan Seasons* 6, no. 3 (Autumn 2003).

Singler, Caroline. "When Thoughts Turn to Springs." *Sagatagan Seasons* 8, no. 2 (Spring 2005): 2, 5.

Sittauer, Kevin. "Everything Old Is New Again." *Sagatagan Seasons* 11, no. 3 (Summer 2008): 3.

Talafous, Don. "A Walk in the Woods." *Saint John's* magazine, 36, no. 1 (Winter 1996): 8.

Tegeder, Vincent. "High Above the Sagatagan: A Landscape Paradise." *The Scriptorium* 25 (1986): 95–107.

"Ten Thousand Norway Pine Trees Planted." *The Record* (April 29, 1932): 2.

Thelen, Lambert. "Ornithological Notes, 1904–08." Saint John's Abbey Archives.

Thimmesh, Hilary. "Reflections." Privately-printed booklet, 1982.

———. *Saint John's at 150.* Collegeville, MN: Saint John's University Press, 2006.

"Thousands of Young Trees Are Planted." *The Record* (May 21, 1925): 3.

Timmerman, Kristina. "Flying Squirrels." *Abbey Banner* (Spring 2014): 22–23.

Tippett, Krista. *Speaking of Faith: Why Religion Matters—and How to Talk About It*. New York: Penguin Books, 2007.

Vogel, Dan. "Morel Season Memories." *Sagatagan Seasons* 7, no. 3 (Summer 2004): 5.

Wienhold, Ron. "Plant of the Season, *Asclepias Syriaca*." *Sagatagan Seasons* 1, no. 3 (Summer 1998): 3.

———. "A Walk in the Woods." *Sagatagan Seasons* 15, no. 1 (Winter 2012): 5.

Wollmering, Bruce. "Avian Observations on Saint John's Campus." *Sagatagan Seasons* 4, no. 3 (Winter 2001): 5.

"Woodsmen Cut Trees for Farm and Evergreen Tracts." *The Record* (March 1, 1928): 3.

Young, Franz. "A Stone House Amongst the Maples: Forestry, Stability, and Benedictinism at Saint John's, 1866–1960." Unpublished manuscript, 2002.

Ziegler, Frank. "Calling Frogs at Saint John's." *Sagatagan Seasons* 4, no. 2 (Summer 2001): 4.

We ourselves seldom comprehend the moment at hand. So we turn to history, the one element of our lives it is possible to fix on. Or we turn to principle. Or we turn to nature. There we find, amid the silence and mystery, order and structure, the sense that life is not simply random.

—Paul Gruchow, *The Necessity of Empty Places*

Contributors

Larry Haeg of Saint Paul, MN, is a retired executive vice president of Wells Fargo & Company, a 1963 graduate of Saint John's Prep, and a 1967 graduate of Saint John's University. He is the author of several books, including *Saint Benedict's Rule for Fair Play in Sports; Harriman vs. Hill: Wall Street's Great Railroad War;* and *In Gatsby's Shadow: The Story of Charles Macomb Flandrau.*

Jennifer Kutter is a 2003 graduate of the College of Saint Benedict. Her degree in chemistry and environmental studies lends itself well to her position as the department coordinator for Saint John's Outdoor University, the Abbey Arboretum, and the CSB/SJU environmental studies department. Kayaking, good music, a little yoga, and spending time with her young daughter feed her soul.

Editorial team:
Hans Christoffersen, publisher for academic and trade markets, Liturgical Press
Ryan Kutter, manager, Saint John's Pottery
Doris Matter, director of communications, Office of the President, SJU
Brother Robin Pierzina, O.S.B., Saint John's Abbey, editor, *Abbey Banner*

The team is grateful for the counsel and contributions of the Rt. Rev. John Klassen, O.S.B., tenth abbot of Saint John's Abbey; Thomas Kroll, director, Saint John's Outdoor University, and land manager, Abbey Arboretum; Peggy Landwehr Roske, archivist, CSB/SJU; cartographer Ben Carlson (SJU '14); Brother David Klingeman, O.S.B., archivist, Saint

John's Abbey; Father Hilary Thimmesh, O.S.B., and Father William Skudlarek, O.S.B., Saint John's Abbey; Dr. Stephen Saupe, professor of biology, CSB/SJU; Paul Beniek, client services, Information Technology Services, CSB/SJU; John Elton, landscape manager, Saint John's University Grounds; Melissa J Bach, environmental education fellow, Saint John's Outdoor University; Taylor Scheele, student intern, Saint John's Outdoor University, CSB '16; and Lauren L. Murphy, Julie Surma, and Colleen Stiller of Liturgical Press.

Trees

I THINK that I shall never see
A poem lovely as a tree.
A tree whose hungry mouth is prest
Against the sweet earth's flowing breast;
A tree that looks at God all day,
And lifts her leafy arms to pray;
A tree that may in summer wear
A nest of robins in her hair;
Upon whose bosom snow has lain;
Who intimately lives with rain.
Poems are made by fools like me,
But only God can make a tree.

—Joyce Kilmer

Photo Credits

Barnes, Dr. Thomas G.; USFWS, 49 (bottom), 82
Barra, A.; commons.wikimedia.org, 47 (top)
Birkhofer, Jenny; Outdoor U, 51 (bottom), 137
Blanda, Stephanie; Outdoor U, 21, 23 (top), 25 (bottom), 46 (top), 197
Bolser, Jessica; USFWS, 103 (top)
Breen, Ann; Outdoor U, 99
Brenny, Christopher; Outdoor U, 44 (bottom), 110 (top)
Brogan, Grace; Outdoor U, 51 (top), 56, 60, 183
Calibas; commons.wikimedia.org, 107
Cameron, Donald; gobotany.newenglandwild.org, 104 (top)
Carlson, Aaron; Flickr, 141
Carlson, Benjamin; Outdoor U, 16, 40, 64, 94, 130, 154
Celley, Courtney; USFWS, 102 (bottom)
Cerulea, Dendrioca; Flickr, 135 (top)
Chang, Gary; Flickr, 143 (top)
Cofell-Dwyer, Liam P.; Outdoor U, 34, 83
Colgan Azar, Kelly; Flickr, 113 (bottom), 147 (top)
College of Saint Benedict Archives, 93
Cook, Bill; Michigan State University; Bugwood.org, vii, ix, 188
Couperus, Jutze; Flickr, 52 (bottom)
Deal, Patrick; Outdoor U, 97 (top)
Delfs, Katelynne; Outdoor U, 42 (top), 74
Durand Demarais, Carla; Outdoor U, 59 (bottom), 67
Eggermont, Theo; Outdoor U, 61
Enking, Leonora; Flickr, 164 (top)

MacGillivray, Matt; Flickr, 170 (bottom)

Marshall, Brett; Sault College; Bugwood.org, 100 (top)

Mayer, Joshua; Flickr, 77 (bottom)

Medvecz, Erin; Outdoor U, 20

Miller, John; Outdoor U, 156 (top)

Moquin, Jamie; Outdoor U, 23 (bottom)

Mueller, Lauren; Outdoor U, 86

Murch, Beatrice; Flickr, 75 (top)

National Park Service, 31 (top), 178

Nierengarten, Lauren; Outdoor U, 65

O'Brien, Joseph; USDA Forest Service; Bugwood.org, 104 (bottom), 195

O'Neal, Alex; Flickr, 169 (top)

Outdoor U Archives, 8, 17 (top), 41, 42 (bottom), 50, 53 (bottom), 72 (top), 81 (top), 116, 144, 181

Pennsylvania Army National Guard; Flickr, 52

Peroutky, Tony; Outdoor U, 24 (bottom), 27 (bottom), 35 (bottom), 45, 49 (top), 55 (top), 73 (bottom), 97 (bottom), 102 (top), 114

Petroglyph; Flickr, 113 (top)

Pierzina, O.S.B., Robin, 127

Pitillo, Dan; USFWS, 103 (bottom)

Pohs, Robert; USFWS, 81 (bottom)

Pollard, Jenna; Outdoor U, 162 (bottom)

Price, Homer Edward, 138 (top)

Rae, S.; Flickr, 30

Ramey, Vic; University of Florida/IFAS Center for Aquatic and Invasive Plants. Used by permission, 73 (top)

Rawlins, Karan A.; forestryimages.org, 140

Round, Emily G.; Flickr, 163

Routledge, Rob; Sault College; Bugwood.org, 101, 131 (top)

Ryden, Hope, 168

Sabae, Andrew; Lake and Wetland Ecosystems. Permission pending, 76

Saint Benedict's Monastery Archives, 93

Saint John's Abbey Archives, ix, 38, 59 (top), 87, 88, 125, 133, 134 (top), 151, 152, 153, 176

Saint John's University Archives, 120

Schechter, Greg; Flickr, 145 (bottom)

Scheele, Taylor; Outdoor U, 46 (bottom), 48, 75 (bottom), 138 (bottom), 142, 164 (bottom), 165 (top), 180

Schmitz, Allen; Outdoor U, 25 (top)

Schwamberger, Benjamin; Outdoor U, 201

Sieh, Bryan; Outdoor U, 148–49

Small, Dave; Flickr, 110 (bottom)

Smith, Wendell; Flickr, 160 (bottom)

Steiger-Meister, Katie; USFWS, 139 (top)

The Saint John's Bible, 9

Tong, Jennifer; Outdoor U, 18

USFWS, 33 (top), 55 (bottom), 80 (bottom), 103 (bottom)

USFWS-Midwest, 79

Virens; Flickr, 100 (bottom)

Volkers, Gabrielle; Outdoor U, 33 (bottom)

Wegner, Paul, 156

Weiss, Megan; Outdoor U, 132 (top)

Westmoreland, Andrea; Flickr, 147 (bottom)

Williss, David; Flickr, 112

Wolf Ridge Environmental Learning Center, 111 (bottom)

Yun Huang Yong; Flickr, 167

Zehowski, Brian; Saint John's Pottery, 121

Index